Exploring Water with Young Children

Trainer's Guide

THE YOUNG SCIENTIST SERIES

Building Structures with Young Children
Building Structures with Young Children Trainer's Guide
Building Structures with Young Children Trainer's Set (Guide and DVD)

Discovering Nature with Young Children
Discovering Nature with Young Children Trainer's Guide
Discovering Nature with Young Children Trainer's Set (Guide and DVD)

Exploring Water with Young Children
Exploring Water with Young Children Trainer's Guide
Exploring Water with Young Children Trainer's Set (Guide and DVD)

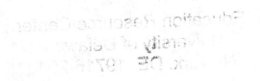

exploring water with young children

Ingrid Chalufour and Karen Worth
Education Development Center, Inc.

The
*Young
Scientist*
Series

Redleaf Press®
www.redleafpress.org
800-423-8309

62789

Published by Redleaf Press
10 Yorkton Court
St. Paul, MN 55117
www.redleafpress.org

Written by Ingrid Chalufour and Karen Worth, with Robin Moriarty, Jeff Winokur, and Sharon Grollman

Printed in the United States of America
17 16 15 14 13 12 11 10   3 4 5 6 7 8 9 10

This book was written with the support of National Science Foundation Grant ESI-9818737. However, any opinions, findings, conclusions, and/or recommendations herein are those of the authors and do not necessarily reflect the views of NSF.

ISBN 978-1-929610-55-6

Printed on acid-free paper

The Young Scientist Series was developed by a team of early childhood and science educators from the Tool Kit for Early Childhood Science Education project at Education Development Center, Inc. (EDC) and was funded by a grant from the National Science Foundation. The project was led by Ingrid Chalufour from the Center for Children and Families and Karen Worth from the Center for Science Education. Listed below are the key members of the team, all of whom contributed substantially to the work from its conceptualization to the final product.

INGRID CHALUFOUR has designed and conducted professional development programs for staff in child care programs, Head Start, public schools, and social service agencies for more than thirty-five years.

SHARON GROLLMAN, a senior research associate at EDC's Center for Children and Families, has developed educational materials for more than twenty years. Prior to coming to EDC, she was part of a research team in early childhood.

ROBIN MORIARTY is a research associate at EDC's Center for Science Education. Her work includes curriculum development, leading professional development programs, and working with early childhood centers. She taught young children in the Boston area for fourteen years before she joined EDC.

JEFFREY WINOKUR is a senior research associate at EDC's Center for Science Education. His work includes curriculum development and leading professional development programs for early childhood and elementary science education. He has worked in early childhood and science education for over twenty years and is an instructor in education at Wheelock College.

KAREN WORTH is a senior scientist at EDC's Center for Science Education. Her work includes the development of science curriculum and professional development programs, as well as consultation in science education for young children. She is also a graduate-level instructor at Wheelock College in the early childhood education department and has worked in the field of science and early childhood education for the past thirty-five years.

contents

acknowledgments

The Young Scientist Series was developed by the project staff of the Tool Kit for Early Childhood Science Education housed at Education Development Center, Inc. (EDC), with funding from the National Science Foundation.

Numerous educators and consultants contributed to the development and field testing of the series. We would like to thank the following people for their contributions to this work.

DEVELOPMENT TEACHERS

Cindy Hoisington
Lucia McAlpin
Carole Moyer
Rebecca Palacios
Susan Steinsick

PILOT TEACHERS

Colette Auguste
Liana Bond
Imelda DeCosta
Marlene Dure
Frank Greene
Karen Hoppe
Terry Küchenmeister
Stuart Lui
Maureen McIntee
Susan Miller
Katherine O'Leary
Carolyn Robinson
Ellen Sulek
Laurie Wormstead
Tiffany Young

FIELD TEST SITES

Bainbridge Island Child Care Centers, Bainbridge Island, WA
Barre Town School, Barre, VT
Berlin Elementary School, Berlin, VT
Blackwater Community School, Coolidge, AZ
Blue Hill Avenue Early Education Center, Boston, MA

Bright Horizons at Preston Corners, Cary, NC
Childspace Day Care Centers, Philadelphia, PA
City of Phoenix Head Start, Phoenix, AZ
Cisco Family Connection Bright Horizons, Milpitas, CA
East Montpelier Elementary School, East Montpelier, VT
Epic Head Start, Yakima, WA
Fort Worth Museum of Science and History, Fort Worth, TX
Four Corners School, East Montpelier, VT
K–5 Inquiry-Based Science Program, Seattle Public Schools, WA
Louisiana Tech University Early Childhood Education Center, Ruston, LA
Motorola Childcare and Education Center, Schaumburg, IL
Pasadena Unified School District, Pasadena, CA
Phoenix Head Start, Phoenix, AZ
Portage Private Industry Council Head Start, Ravenna, OH
School for Early Learning, Spring Branch Independent School District, Houston, TX
Thomson Early Childhood Center, Seattle, WA
UMC Child Development Lab, Columbia, MO

Valle Imperial Project in Science, El Centro, CA
William H. Rowe School, Yarmouth, ME
Young Achievers Science and Mathematics Pilot School, Boston, MA

ADVISORY BOARD MEMBERS

Douglas Clements
David Dickinson
George Forman
Linda French
Marilou Hyson
Stephanie Johnson
Diane Levin
Mary Jane Moran
Carolyn Vieria
Sandra Williams
Diane Willow

CONSULTANTS

Mary Eisenberg
Pat Fitzsimmons
Ben Mardell
Janet Sebell

We also would like to acknowledge the following people at EDC:

Erica Fields, Research Assistant
Kerry Ouellet, Editor and Production Manager
Susan Weinberg, Senior Administrative Assistant

introduction

"The Young Scientist professional development materials were very, very helpful. As an instructor I knew just what to do and the teachers really enjoyed the workshops. I feel their excitement has transferred to the children. Both boys and girls are interested in and excited about their science explorations."

—EARLY CARE AND EDUCATION PROGRAM DIRECTOR

Cindy Richards, director of the West Side Early Childhood Center, found that the current trends toward standards and child outcomes caused her to question what children were really learning. Teachers were concentrating on helping children to recognize letters, rather than encouraging children to look at books or use print to communicate their own ideas. Her teachers would set up a science table, but children rarely spent time there or investigated a topic in-depth. Ms. Richards had been sending teachers to workshops for years—hoping her teachers would learn new strategies for improving early literacy, science, and math—but the effects were rarely apparent in the classroom. Ms. Richards felt the time had come to change her approach, but she was unsure what she could do to improve teaching and learning in her program.

Then she was asked if her program would field-test the Young Scientist teacher guides—on water, living things, and structures—and the accompanying professional development program. Ms. Richards was reluctant at first, wondering if this was just one more gimmick, just one more shot in the dark. Flipping through the materials, she was surprised to see how extensive the program was—which was a bit daunting. But she hoped the comprehensive nature of this approach might lead to the changes she was looking for. So she said yes. She found that the hands-on exploration built teachers' understanding of the science content, inquiry process, and the Young Scientist approach to teaching. The video vignettes helped teachers connect this content approach to their own teaching practice. Ms. Richards notes, "One of the most important things I learned was that it takes time to learn new approaches and integrate them into teaching practice. It takes time to provide teachers with the ongoing support they need to sustain successful change."

As a result of participating in this professional development program, Ms. Richards sees evidence of teachers applying what they have learned. Teachers are engaging children in in-depth science explorations over time. Teachers' conversations with children don't just focus on management now (such as "Make sure not to spill on the floor"), but on what children are doing and thinking (such as "How could you make the water flow through this tube?"). For the first time, many teachers are documenting children's observations and ideas and using them to extend learning. This has been evident not only in science, but in other domains as well. Ms. Richards reflects, "Teachers see their role, their curriculum, and the children in a new way. For the first time, they are recognizing and capitalizing on the science in the everyday, which helps them to guide children's science learning more effectively. At the same time, they appreciate what children notice and wonder about, what they can do, and understand."

Others who have field-tested the Young Scientist Series have had similar reactions:

"I found it really easy to follow. Everything was very clear. Anybody could use it. The teachers didn't lose interest. They really liked the hands-on parts, and they were very engaged in the reflective discussions."
—PUBLIC SCHOOL ADMINISTRATOR

"When I read through the workshops, they looked so good, I decided we needed to do them all!"
—HEAD START DIRECTOR

The Young Scientist

The above vignette suggests the excitement that can be generated when teachers really enjoy learning about and trying out new teaching approaches. In order to build the knowledge and skills teachers need to implement an inquiry-based science curriculum, the Young Scientist provides both teacher guides and a comprehensive set of training materials for each of three science explorations:

- *Discovering Nature with Young Children* invites children to assume the role of a naturalist as they observe and learn about plants and animals in the immediate outdoors, as well as in their own classrooms.

- *Building Structures with Young Children* engages children in investigating the relationships between building materials and design and the strength and stability of the structures.

- *Exploring Water with Young Children* helps children examine the properties of water.

DEVELOPMENT AND TESTING

The Young Scientist is a result of a four-year grant funded by the National Science Foundation. It draws on current understanding of best practice in science teaching and learning. Key to the development process has been the involvement of practitioners and experts from the field who have helped us design the approach, review draft documents, and test the curriculum and professional development materials. The final stage in this process was a national field test conducted from 2001 and 2002, in nineteen early childhood programs including Head Start, pre-K, child care centers, and private nursery schools. Program directors, education managers, and curriculum coordinators from these programs planned and implemented the training activities. Ninety teachers participated in the workshops and used the teacher's guide in their classrooms. Results revealed that some combination of the workshops and more informal support was important to help teachers apply their new learning in the classroom. Moreover, participants reported evidence of science learning in children's questions, observations, and discussions.

Overview of the Trainer's Guide

Teachers often feel insecure and inadequate about their own understanding of science concepts and do not realize how they can learn through inquiry and then use their new understanding in the classroom. These training materials focus on helping teachers begin to gain an understanding of the underlying science concepts in the *Exploring Water with Young Children* teacher's guide and to learn to use that guide to facilitate children's inquiry into properties of water.

This guide includes all of the instructions, print, and video materials you will need to provide rich professional development experiences for your teachers as they implement the *Exploring Water with Young Children* teacher's guide in their classrooms. When workshops and guided discussions are combined with mentoring over time, your training program will lead to a quality science education program.

The trainer's guide has four components:

- A set of seven **BASIC WORKSHOPS:** These workshops use hands-on experiences and reflective conversations to provide teachers with the following: a practical understanding of the science content and inquiry process that will inform their teaching; help in recognizing the science in children's work; and help in guiding children's explorations. These workshops also provide an overview of all sections of the teacher's guide.

- Eight **ADVANCED WORKSHOPS:** These workshops use samples of children's work and conversations to help teachers build a practical understanding of their multifaceted role as facilitators of science inquiry.

- A structure for **GUIDED DISCUSSIONS:** These discussions provide a forum for small groups of teachers to use classroom documentation to stimulate collaborative reflection on their own science teaching and plan new and more effective approaches.

- A description of a **MENTORING PROGRAM:** This section helps mentors use classroom observations and conferencing to support teachers with their individual challenges and help them assess their teaching and refine their practice.

The following sections will help you plan and implement your program:

- **PLANNING AN EFFECTIVE PROFESSIONAL DEVELOPMENT PROGRAM** (below) will help you select the appropriate components and schedule your events.

- **GETTING STARTED** (p. 6) describes a three-step process for preparing yourself for conducting the basic and advanced workshops.

- **RESOURCES** (p. 193) offers a range of tools, including descriptions of each of the instructional strategies used in the workshops, guidance and forms for evaluating teacher growth and planning guided discussions, a log of the video vignettes, and a bibliography of readings for you and for teachers.

Planning an Effective Professional Development Program

These comprehensive training materials, designed to support teacher implementation of the *Exploring Water with Young Children* teacher's guide, can be adapted to the needs of your particular program and teachers. We suggest you plan a three-stage program.

1. Help teachers become familiar with the teacher's guide and the science concepts and inquiry process at the heart of *Exploring Water with Young Children*.

2. Help teachers build their capacity as inquiry-based science teachers.

3. Sustain progress you have made and support teachers as they continue to refine their science teaching practice.

Implement these stages one at a time, based on your assessment of teachers' strengths and needs.

STAGE 1: LEARN TO USE THE TEACHER'S GUIDE

Use the seven basic workshops to help teachers understand the exploring water science concepts, the inquiry process, and the teacher's guide. These workshops, which consist of one three-hour introduction and six one-and-a-half-hour sessions, provide the knowledge and experience teachers need as they begin to implement the teacher's guide. When scheduling the workshops consider several factors:

- Teachers will need the first three workshops before they begin using *Exploring Water with Young Children* in the classroom. These workshops will introduce the science concepts and the nature of science inquiry, help them prepare their environment, and provide an overview of open exploration.

- Teachers will need workshops 4 and 5 before moving on to focused exploration in the classroom. These two workshops will provide a hands-on focused exploration and an overview of the purpose and teacher role in this stage of children's exploration, preparing them to facilitate deeper investigations. Try not to wait more than three weeks between workshops 3 and 4. Teachers will need to understand how to deepen children's investigation and apply this in the classroom, otherwise the children will lose interest.

- Find ways to keep this focus on science teaching and learning in the foreground of your program's activity. Check in with teachers regularly to see how things are going in their classrooms. Do they have the materials they need? Are they finding enough time for exploration and science talks? Are the children engaged? Use mentoring or guided discussions to maintain the focus if there are extended periods between the workshops.

PROGRAM SAMPLE SCHEDULES:

1. The teachers in the sample program were able to schedule most of their training sessions during naptime when they would otherwise be planning. They were also able to fit in a full-day session before the school year began. The director wanted to provide individual support from the beginning by scheduling two observation and conferencing sessions with each teacher during stage 1. The first helped teachers make the transition to focused exploration. The second supported their efforts to integrate representation and science talks into their regular routine and to use them effectively for science learning.

SCIENCE EXPLORATIONS WORKSHOP SCHEDULE

September 3
9:00 A.M.–3:00 P.M.
Workshops 1 and 2: Introduction and
Getting Ready

September 12
1:30–3:00 P.M.
Workshop 3: Open Exploration

Observation and conferences will be scheduled with each classroom from September 26
through October 10.

October 3
1:30–3:00 P.M.
Workshop 4: Focused Exploration of Flow

October 10
1:30–3:00 P.M.
Workshop 5: Overview of Focused Exploration

Observation and conferences will be scheduled with each teacher from October 10
through November 7.

November 7
1:00–2:30 P.M.
Workshop 6: Focused Exploration of Drops

December 12
1:00–2:30 P.M.
Workshop 7: Focused Exploration of Sinking
and Floating

2. In another center there is no time during the day for workshops, but the teachers were eager to implement the program in their classrooms. The director offered pizza dinner and baby-sitting in exchange for their participation after the center closed. The director did her first observation and conference at the end of the series to help her prepare for stage 2.

HIGHLAND CHILD CARE CENTER'S SCIENCE EXPLORATIONS WORKSHOPS

Everybody Attend!!!
Pizza served at 6:30 P.M.
Workshops begin promptly at 7:00 P.M.

September 4*, 11, 18; October 9, 16; November 13, 20

*Note: The September 4 workshop is 6:00–9:00 P.M.

STAGE 2: BUILD CAPACITY AS INQUIRY-BASED SCIENCE TEACHERS

If you have completed the basic workshops, teachers should be beginning to use the guide and this approach to engaging children in exploring water. Use "Assessing Teacher Growth" (in "Resources," p. 203) to assess their practice. Work with the teachers to identify appropriate goals. "Science Teacher Development Plan" ("Resources," p. 211) is a useful resource when you are considering next steps and the level of support to provide as you move on. Teachers still at the beginning stage might need some help, individually or in a small group, with the goals that best meet their needs. The chapters on mentoring and guided discussion will help you plan your work with them.

Many teachers will be ready to move on to the advanced workshops after completing the basic ones. As you plan consider the following:

- Start with the first advanced workshop, "Creating a Culture of Inquiry about Water," which includes an individual needs assessment that will help you better understand how the teachers perceive their needs and interests.

- Plan a sequence of workshops that best reflects the needs and interests identified by the teachers and you.

- Allow time in between workshops (at least one month) for teachers to implement the approaches presented.

- Use mentoring or guided discussions to support teachers' efforts in between the workshops.

STAGE 3: PROVIDE ONGOING SUPPORT AS TEACHERS REFINE THEIR PRACTICE

If you have not used guided discussions and mentoring before completing the basic and advanced workshops, now is the time. Regular opportunities to talk about science teaching and learning will be key to sustaining and building on the gains you have made. Guided discussions provide a vehicle for encouraging documentation and analysis of the teaching and learning going on in your program. At the same time, you will be encouraging teacher collaboration and providing a vehicle for analysis and refining science teaching. Mentoring is also an important way to help teachers progress by addressing their interests and concerns directly in relation to their classroom. Use the chapters on guided discussion and mentoring to plan this stage of your professional development program.

Getting Started

The time you spend preparing will contribute to the success of your professional development events. Here we describe the special things you can do to prepare for the workshops. Follow these steps as you get ready:

1. Become familiar with the teacher's and trainer's guides.

2. Find a location for the workshops.

3. Prepare to be an instructor.

STEP 1: BECOME FAMILIAR WITH THE TEACHER'S AND TRAINER'S GUIDES

A clear understanding of the curriculum and its science content will be essential if you are to help others understand this approach to teaching and learning. Carefully read the teacher's guide, familiarizing yourself with its approach and structure. Consider what aspects of this approach will be familiar to teachers and which ones will be new. Identify the parts of the guide that will be particularly helpful to teachers. Reading the guide more than once will help you build your own understanding of this teaching method and the various ways the guide supports teacher adoption.

Next, familiarize yourself with these professional development materials. Quickly reading the whole package will give you the big picture—an overview of the structure and content of the instructions and the supporting materials. In a more focused read, examine each aspect of the instructional approach and anticipate how teachers might respond.

STEP 2: FIND A LOCATION FOR THE WORKSHOPS

Select sites for your workshops that will be comfortable and provide easy access to water tables and water. Easy availability of an overhead projector, screen, VCR, and monitor will make your work easier.

STEP 3: PREPARE TO BE AN INSTRUCTOR

Familiarity with both content and process of the workshops will give you confidence as a presenter. Take the time to complete these tasks.

- Explore the water concepts using the guidance in basic workshop 1 and in the "Getting Ready" section of the teacher's guide (p. 13). In addition, do the hands-on activities that are described in basic workshops 4, 6, and 7. The science is complicated and it is important that you work with these concepts in advance, build your understanding, and decide just how much you are prepared to talk about each of them when working with teachers.

- Think through the discussion questions, answering them for yourself. Try to anticipate how teachers will react and then imagine your responses.

- Preview the video vignettes that you will be showing. As you watch, think about the purpose of the vignettes, children's engagement with science, the science teaching strategies they illustrate, and what you want teachers to gain from the viewing and conversation.

- Collect the materials. Review the lists early (see the section on advance preparation for each workshop) and make plans for how you will get all of these things before the day of the workshop. Suggestions for finding many of these items can be found in the "Resources" section in the teacher's guide (p. 105).

- Prepare the handouts and overheads. For the most part, you will refer participants to the resources in the teacher's guide, but there are a few handouts in the professional development package that provide guidance for small group work or observation of videos. These handouts appear at the end of the instructions for each workshop. Each participant will need a copy of each handout. The final handout is an evaluation that all participants should complete at the end of the basic or advanced workshops. The overheads, found at the end of both workshop sections, give the content a visual aid. You will need to copy them onto transparencies.

- Consider how you want to handle the "Read and Reflect" pre-assignments, which have been included for each of the basic workshops. You will need to copy and distribute them to teachers at least a week before each session. These assignments include readings in the teacher's guide and reflection questions. Completing the assignments will ensure that teachers are familiar with the content of each session and ready to participate fully in the discussions. You will probably want to collect teachers' responses and review their reflections to gain insight into teachers' understandings. This will help you tailor sessions to meet the needs of individual teachers.

- Review key instructional strategies in "Resources," which will help you effectively use the various teaching strategies in these workshops.

basic workshops

The seven workshops are designed to familiarize teachers with the teacher's guide and the underlying science content. They include the following:

- Workshop 1: Introduction to *Exploring Water with Young Children*—Teachers learn about the science content and inquiry skills at the heart of *Exploring Water with Young Children*.
- Workshop 2: Getting Ready—Teachers prepare a science-rich environment for children's water investigations.
- Workshop 3: Overview of Open Exploration—Teachers are introduced to the purpose and flow of open exploration.
- Workshop 4: Focused Exploration of Flow—Teachers deepen their understanding of key science concepts and inquiry skills, as well as their approach to teaching and learning, through a hands-on exploration of controlling water's flow.
- Workshop 5: Overview of Focused Exploration—Teachers are introduced to the purpose and flow of focused exploration, and share their own classroom observations.
- Workshop 6: Focused Exploration of Drops—Teachers explore the behavior of drops of water and further their understanding of the science and this approach to teaching and learning.
- Workshop 7: Focused Exploration of Sinking and Floating—In this 1½-hour session, teachers learn how they can explore sinking and floating with young children with a focus on the underlying science concepts.

Each workshop includes the following sections:

- At a Glance—purpose, activities, timeline, materials, and pre-assignment for each session
- Objectives—what you want teachers to gain by the end of the session
- Overview—activity descriptions and suggestions for time management
- Instructor Preparation—materials needed and steps to take to get ready for each session
- Detailed step-by-step instructions
- Handouts to copy for each teacher
- Overheads to copy as transparencies before each session
- "Read and Reflect" pre-assignments to copy and distribute at least a week before each session

You can also refer to the key instructional strategies in "Resources" (see p. 193) to help you prepare and conduct the basic workshops.

Introduction to
Exploring Water with Young Children

AT A GLANCE

Purpose:
- Gain beginning understanding of this approach to teaching and learning in the early childhood classroom.
- Begin to understand the science concepts and inquiry skills.
- Learn about the teacher's guide and how it is organized.

Activity	Time: 3 hours	Materials
Introduction Introduce teachers to the basic workshops and the teacher's guide. Use a video vignette to show the program "in action." Invite teachers to share any previous experiences with water.	55 minutes	• Handouts: agenda, "Read and Reflect 1" • Copies of *Exploring Water with Young Children* teacher's guides • Self-adhesive note pads • VCR, monitor, and video cued to vignette 1 • Overhead projector, screen, and overhead 1.1
Water Flow Exploration Facilitate an exploration of water flow. Model the role that teachers will play with children by encouraging engagement and focusing on the properties of water.	1 hour 10 minutes	• Materials for exploring water • Books about water • Posters or pictures of water flow • Charts: "What We Notice about Water" and "What We Notice about the Materials" • Camera and film or digital camera (optional)
The Science Introduce the science concepts and inquiry process, and help teachers connect them to their own water experiences.	55 minutes	• Overhead projector, screen, and overheads 1.2 and 1.3 • Copies of "Read and Reflect 2"

Pre-assignment: Read introduction to *Exploring Water with Young Children* and excerpts from a teacher's journal and respond to reflection questions.

Basic Workshop 1: Introduction

OBJECTIVES

- Gain beginning understanding of this approach to teaching and learning in the early childhood classroom.
- Begin to understand the science concepts and inquiry skills.
- Learn about the teacher's guide and how it is organized.

OVERVIEW

- Introduction (55 minutes)
- Water flow exploration (1 hour 10 minutes)
- The science (55 minutes)

INSTRUCTOR PREPARATION

- Distribute "Read and Reflect 1" with the teacher's guide at least one week before the workshop. Ask teachers to complete the assignment before the first workshop.
- Prepare an agenda that outlines the seven basic workshops, as well as where and when they will take place.
- Prepare the materials for the exploration. You will need a variety of materials, listed below, and water tables or tubs for small groups of teachers. Refer to the resources section of the teacher's guide for advice about finding and setting up the water materials. Select a convenient place for the session. This activity will be easiest if you are near a source of water. Have supplies on hand to clean any spilled water.
- Review step 1 of open exploration in the teacher's guide in preparation for facilitating the exploration. The exploration will model the approach described in the open exploration section of the teacher's guide. The exploration described in this workshop differs from the teacher's guide in that it is designed to help adults learn about the properties of water in preparation for teaching young children. It is not an exact replication of the approach to use with children.
- Review "Step 1: Preparing Yourself—Science" in the "Getting Ready" section of the teacher's guide (p. 13) in preparation for talking with teachers about science concepts.
- Preview video vignette 1. As you look at the video, find the teacher and child actions that exemplify the points you want to make about this approach. The instructions that follow provide suggestions.

MATERIALS

- Handouts: agenda, "Read and Reflect" 1 and 2
- *Exploring Water with Young Children* teacher's guides for each teacher
- Materials for exploring water (see the resources section in the teacher's guide for a description of materials), such as: large container (at least 10 by 15 by 9 inches), about ½ to ⅔

filled with water (this can include one standard-size water table); three or four small, clear plastic containers of various shapes and sizes for pouring and containing water (such as recycled plastic bottles, cups, and measuring cups); one or two clear plastic pump bottles (such as those for liquid soap); three pieces of clear flexible tubing of different diameters (one piece of ¼-inch inner diameter [ID], one piece of ⅜-inch ID, one piece of ½-inch ID), cut to ½- to 2-foot lengths; one or two turkey basters that can fit into at least one of the pieces of tubing; two funnels that can fit into at least one of the pieces of tubing; one kerosene or bilge pump; two or three T- or Y-connectors that can fit into at least one of the pieces of tubing

- Wire water wall (see the resources section in the teacher's guide for a description)
- Books about water
- Posters or pictures of water flow
- Small self-adhesive note pads for each teacher
- Charts: "What We Notice about Water" and "What We Notice about the Materials"
- Camera and film or digital camera (optional)
- Overhead projector, screen, and overheads 1.1–1.3
- Video cued to vignette 1, VCR, and monitor

For the first fifteen minutes of the exploration, provide all materials listed above except for the following:

- T- and Y-connectors
- Wire water wall

Activity

Introduction (55 minutes)

Purpose:

- To set the stage by introducing the curriculum, its vision for science teaching and learning, and the nature of the work teachers will be doing with you during the workshops
- To uncover what teachers already know about water, how it moves, and some of its other properties

1. **Give a short presentation** (5 minutes) that provides teachers with a brief overview of the workshops. Distribute the agenda and review it with teachers, being explicit about any requirements for their participation in the workshops and use of the curriculum. Tell them they will be learning about the following:

   - How to use the *Exploring Water with Young Children* teacher's guide to explore water over time with children
   - Science concepts and inquiry skills of water exploration
   - The teacher's role in facilitating children's inquiry and science learning

2. INTRODUCE THE TEACHER'S GUIDE AND THE "READ AND REFLECT" ASSIGNMENTS (10 minutes). Tell teachers that the guide provides information and direction for conducting an investigation of water that can take place over several months. Mention that the read and reflect assignments are meant to introduce them to the teacher's guide and can be used to prepare for each workshop. Explain that you will refer them back to sections of the guide during the session and suggest that they use the self-adhesive notes to mark pages that are discussed for easy reference.

3. USE VIGNETTE 1 TO INTRODUCE *EXPLORING WATER WITH YOUNG CHILDREN* (30 minutes).

    a. Begin by using overhead 1.1 to review the guiding principles listed in the introduction. Suggest that teachers look for these things as they watch the video.

OVERHEAD 1.1: *EXPLORING WATER WITH YOUNG CHILDREN* GUIDING PRINCIPLES

- All three- to five-year-olds can successfully experience rich, in-depth scientific inquiry.
- The science content draws from children's experiences, is interesting and engaging, and can be explored directly and deeply over time.
- Expectations are developmentally appropriate; that is, they are realistic and can be tailored to the strengths, interests, and needs of individual children.
- Discussion, expression, and representation are critical ways in which children reflect on and develop theories from their active work.
- Children learn from one another.
- Teachers take on specific roles to actively support and guide children's science learning.

---

    b. Introduce the vignette by saying that one classroom from a Boston Head Start, one from a Connecticut childcare program, and three Boston kindergartens are shown. The children are all three, four, and five years old and engaged in a water exploration. Show the vignette, asking the teachers to note examples of the guiding principles at work.

    c. Ask for reactions using these questions: "Did you see anything that reminded you of a guiding principle? What did you see and which principle did it exemplify?" You might also want to discuss how the teachers in the vignette compare to teachers A, B, and C in the introduction to the teacher's guide. Ask for specifics.

Make these points about the vignette and this approach to teaching and learning.

- The children seem engaged and excited about exploring water.
- Children are able to engage at varied levels of ability.
- Representation and conversation provide important opportunities to reflect and draw meaning from water explorations.
- The teacher is key in the process of engaging in inquiry and using experiences to gain a deeper understanding of science ideas.

When discussing how the teachers in the vignette compare to teacher C, be sure to highlight the following:

- They are building on interests expressed in children's water play.
- Hands-on experiences combined with dialogue and representation promote learning key science concepts.
- They use carefully selected materials that encourage children to explore the properties of water and how it moves.
- The teachers guide inquiry, encouraging close observation and representation, and helping with data collection and analysis.

4. **DISCUSS TEACHERS' DAILY EXPERIENCES WITH WATER** (10 minutes). Mention that we all experience water every day. Encourage a few people to talk about how water is important in their lives. After participants share their experiences for a few minutes, help them think about how water moves. Accept all comments. This is not a time to talk about the underlying science; it is just an exercise to help teachers feel comfortable with the topic.

Use the following questions to guide the discussion:

- What are some of the ways water is important in your lives?
- What are the different ways you have used water?
- What have you noticed about the different ways water moves?
- Have you ever wondered what makes water go up, down, fast, or slow?

It is important for learners to talk about what they already know. Making the connections to their knowledge and everyday experiences acknowledges their value and helps them integrate new information. In this case, it can ease them into science by helping them realize science is already a part of their lives.

WATER FLOW EXPLORATION (1 HOUR 10 MINUTES)

PURPOSE: Through the process of engaging teachers in a water exploration you will achieve the following:

- Provide a beginning experience with inquiry and the science content on which you will build throughout the workshops
- Reinforce the importance of having firsthand experience using different materials to explore water flow
- Model the teacher's role in facilitating scientific explorations
- Model a science talk that helps teachers build on one another's understanding

1. **INTRODUCE THE WATER FLOW EXPLORATION WITH A CHART** (5 minutes) by saying that they will spend some time exploring some of the materials and science concepts relating to water flow. Tell them that this activity will include some open-ended exploration and some time when they will try some specific things. Begin the exploration by showing teachers each material they will use to explore water.

Ask the teachers to form groups of three or four. Tell them to spend the next ten minutes finding out how to use the different materials to explore water. Also ask them to pay attention to the water itself. Keep group size as small as you can to increase engagement. Tell teachers that you will be modeling the kinds of interactions they should have with their children during their early water explorations. Ask them to pay attention to your comments and questions and note how they influence their work and thinking.

For this portion of the exploration, provide all materials listed above except for the following:

- T- and Y-connectors
- Wire water wall

2. **HELP TEACHERS GET STARTED** (10 minutes). As teachers explore the materials and water in an open-ended way, walk around the room and observe what they are doing. As teachers become engaged, encourage them to describe what they notice. Make comments or ask questions that encourage people to be descriptive, such as the following:

- When pouring from one container to another of a different size—"Notice the height of the water in each container. Before you pour, predict how high the water will go into the new container."

- When connecting a funnel to tubing and pouring into the funnel—"What do you think would happen if you put your finger over the end of the tubing and then poured the water into the funnel?"

- "What do you think would happen if you connected a piece of tubing to the baster?"

3. **BRING THE TEACHERS TOGETHER FOR A TEN-MINUTE SCIENCE TALK.** Ask the teachers to stop their exploration for a moment to discuss briefly what they've noticed about the materials and the water itself. Ask probing questions to get specific comments about their observations. List people's observation on the charts, "What We Notice about Water" and "What We Notice about the Materials."

4. **FACILITATE AN EXPLORATION OF WATER FLOW WITH THE WIRE WATER WALL** (30 minutes). Introduce the wire water wall and the T- and Y-connectors. Demonstrate how the connectors fit into the tubing so it is possible to have more than one stream of water flowing at a time. Demonstrate how the tubing can be passed through or attached to the water wall, freeing up their hands. Tell teachers that these materials are being added as a way for them to support the tubing and expand the possibilities for their water flow explorations. Ask them to use these materials to make water flow in as many ways as possible.

As teachers return to their explorations, make sure each small group is using its time well. Connect the work of two groups if one needs encouragement. Facilitate their experience by trying the following:

- Encourage teachers to try connecting the tubing together with the T- or Y-connectors.

- Encourage teachers to find different ways to move the water.

- Help teachers identify questions they want to investigate.

- Suggest teachers document their work and findings by taking notes, making drawings, or writing down bits of conversation.

5. **FACILITATE A LARGE GROUP SCIENCE TALK** (15 minutes). Bring teachers together and ask questions that focus on how they use the materials to control water flow. Refer back to the charts, adding new observations.

An example of probing questions:
What were you doing with the tubing? . . . And what happened? . . . Did that surprise you? . . . What did you expect to see?

THE SCIENCE (55 MINUTES)

PURPOSE: Inquiry is a concept that is central to science and should be a part of all science education. Therefore, one of the teacher's primary goals is to help children experience and use the processes of inquiry, integrating them into their daily experiences. The science content is also an important feature of *Exploring Water with Young Children*. It is central to every water experience and conversation. The inquiry and content are introduced here and will be reinforced throughout the workshops.

1. **INTRODUCE THE CONCEPT OF INQUIRY** (10 minutes). Tell teachers that they have been engaged in a part of the process of inquiry and that it is a central idea in science and *Exploring Water with Young Children*. Refer them to the inquiry diagram on p. 96 of the teacher's guide as you show overhead 1.2: Inquiry Diagram. Make the following points as you talk about the diagram:

   - *It is a dynamic process.*
     This process is cyclical in nature. It cannot be fully represented in a linear two-dimensional diagram.

   - *It begins with engagement and wondering.*
     Experience with things, materials, and events is the basis of inquiry. This is a time for play and messing around. At this point, the teachers and children are noticing the characteristics of water, the materials, and what they will do.

   - *Wondering leads to more focused observation and questions.*
     As you explore, you may have lots of questions. "How much water does it take to fill this container? What happens when I get to the top? How much can I get in here with one squeeze?" Some people ask their questions; others may reveal their questions through actions.

   - *Questions focus observation and lead to investigation.*
     In order to pursue something in depth, a single question needs to be identified and refined. There are many kinds of questions. At this point, you and the children need to consider which questions can be answered through simple investigations or which

can be modified and pursued through investigation. Ask predicting questions, such as "What will happen if . . ."

- *Investigation is a cyclical process.*
  Investigations begin with a focus or question: "How can I get the water in the baster? What happens when I connect tubing to the baster? Can I make the water come out of two places?" They involve planning, observing closely, recording experiences, and reflecting in order to identify patterns and construct theories and explanations. New questions arise and are pursued. With your guidance, the children can engage in this experimental stage of inquiry.

- *Share, discuss, reflect, and draw conclusions.*
  This is a time for making meaning of investigations. In small and large groups, you and the children share and form simple ideas and generalizations that will deepen their understanding of the concepts being explored.

2. **REFLECT ON THE ROLE INQUIRY PLAYED IN THEIR EXPLORATION** (15 minutes). Ask teachers what aspects of the diagram describe experiences they had during the exploration. Here are some guiding questions:

- How would you describe the inquiry you just engaged in? Did you experience particular aspects of the diagram during your exploration? What are they?

- Which questions drove your investigation?

- What kind of data did you collect related to your questions? How did you document the data?

Now help them think more analytically about their inquiry:

- Did identifying questions play a role in your exploration of water flow? What role did it play?

- How did you use the data you collected? (Ask for specifics about insights they might have had as they documented.)

- What evidence influenced you to change your thinking?

- When and how did you draw some conclusions?

As you make specific connections between their activity and the diagram, emphasize the following:

- Questions and focused activity grow out of an early period of engagement called open exploration.

- Questions help focus observation and investigations.

- Sharing ideas exposes one to more data and to different perspectives and ideas, and opens new doors for investigation.

- Recording data as it is collected is useful because it provides a reference for analysis.

- Science is grounded in evidence. An important part of inquiry is finding the evidence.

3. **INTRODUCE THE SCIENCE CONCEPTS** (25 minutes) by saying that your questions and comments during their exploration were designed to focus them on particular issues. Direct them to descriptions of the science concepts that appear as "Coming Ready" on p. 16 of the teacher's guide. Be sure to mention, as the teacher's guide does, that you are not recommending that they talk about these concepts with children the same way that they are presented here, but their understanding of these concepts will be important as they observe and facilitate the children's experiences. Suggest marking the page with a self-adhesive note for quick reference. Review overhead 1.3.

OVERHEAD 1.3: SCIENCE CONCEPTS

- **Water flows**
  Water's movement is generally described as flow, and water flows down due to gravity. This can be seen in many different ways—rivers flow from higher places to lower ones, drops of rain flow down windowpanes, streams of rain flow down gutters and downspouts, and water poured slowly from one cup to another will flow to the lower container.

  Water can also be made to move up when the force exerted on it is stronger than the downward pull of gravity, such as when you push on it to squirt it up out of a dropper or syringe. It goes up into a turkey baster or eyedropper, or when you suck on it and air pressure pushes it up a straw. Water moves faster or slower as well, depending on the strength of the forces acting on it.

- **Water takes the shape of its container**
  When water is in a cup, pitcher, tube, bowl, swimming pool, or lake, the surface of the water will be flat unless it is moved by something else (for example, wind or shaking). All parts of the container will be filled with water.

- **Cohesion**
  Water molecules stick together (cohesion). When the amount of the water is small, this property of water causes it to form drops. It is also the cause of surface tension, as water forms a kind of "skin" at its surface. Some bugs, for example, can scoot across the surface of a pond or puddle. If you fill a glass to the top you can keep adding a small amount until it is actually a little more than full. This is also because of surface tension.

- **Adhesion**
  Water sticks to other materials (adhesion). It sticks more or less strongly depending on what the material is. Water does not stick well to waxed paper, so drops are round, but it sticks well to paper towels or newspapers, so drops are pulled apart. This property of water is what makes things wet.

- **Objects can sink, float, or stay suspended in water**
  Whether a solid object will sink, float, or stay suspended in water has to do with the relationship between its density and the density of water. Density is the mass of a substance per unit volume—or we can also say it is the weight per unit volume. Some materials will sink in water in one shape and then float if their shape is changed. (For example, a ball of clay will sink whereas that same amount of clay, if spread out and shaped like a boat, will float.) The ball of clay is denser than water and sinks. But the boat, made out of the same amount of clay (the same mass), is bigger (more volume). Its density is less than the density of water and it floats. Thus, an ocean liner floats, even though it is made of metal. If we took all that metal and made it into a solid ball, it would certainly sink. There are factors other than shape that also can determine whether an object will sink or float in water. For example, some materials such as Styrofoam or many kinds of wood are less dense than water no matter what their shape. Also, some things sink when they are not well balanced because they tip and water comes in.

- **Air takes up space and floats to the top of water**
  Both water and air take up space. In order for water to enter an "empty" cup, funnel, piece of tubing, or turkey baster, it must take the place of the air that was already there. When pouring water into a cup, the air is easily replaced by the water. But it you put a cup under water with its open end down, you have to tip it to let the air out so the water can get in it. You can see the bubbles of air come out. Since air is always less dense than water, those bubbles will quickly float to the top of the water and pop. Sometimes, such as when trying to put water into a narrow piece of tubing that is closed at the bottom, the air in the tubing can't get out the top, allowing no water to get in.

Relate the science concepts to their explorations by reviewing the charts, "What We Notice about Water" and "What We Notice about Materials" and asking them to relate their observations to the science concepts. Encourage participants to come up with an example of how they may have been exposed to that concept during their exploration.

Look for ideas such as the following:

- When I was holding the tubing in a *U* shape, the water level was the same in both parts of the *U*.

- The water would always flow down the tubing, except when I squeezed the baster into the bottom of the tubing—then the water went up.

- I noticed that when I filled up a container all the way, I could even add a little more water to it, so the top seemed to hold together without spilling over.

4. **CONCLUDE THE WORKSHOP** (5 minutes) by telling teachers that they will have more opportunities to engage in and talk about inquiry, the science concepts, and the teaching approach in future workshops. You might want to collect "Read and Reflect 1" to get a better understanding of what teachers are thinking. Thank teachers for their participation. Give them "Read and Reflect 2" and confirm the time and place for the next workshop.

READ AND REFLECT 1: INTRODUCTION TO
EXPLORING WATER WITH YOUNG CHILDREN

Name: _____

Before coming to workshop 1, read the introduction to the teacher's guide and the excerpts from a teacher's journal. Respond to these questions as you reflect on what you read. This information will be helpful in the workshop discussion.

1. As you read about teachers A, B, and C, did you make connections to your own teaching? Which teacher was most like you?

2. What were the similarities?

3. What challenges will you face in learning the approach of teacher C?

READ AND REFLECT 2:
GETTING READY

Name: _____

Before coming to workshop 2, read "Getting Ready" and "Essential Information," as well as the "Books and Web Sites" sections in "Resources" at the back of the teacher's guide. Copy and complete the classroom environment checklist in the appendices. Once it is complete, reflect on the following questions. This information will be helpful in the workshop discussion.

1. What are the strengths of your environment? What important elements do you have for your water exploration?

2. What challenges do you face? What important elements are you missing?

Getting Ready

AT A GLANCE

Purpose:
- Gain understanding of the important elements of a science-rich learning environment
- Assess needs of own environment and plan for adaptations
- Begin to understand how children's water play is connected to science concepts and inquiry skills

Activity	Time: 1½ hours	Materials
Overview of Water Environment Discuss important elements of an environment that encourage an exploration of water, using photos for analysis.	30 minutes	• Overhead projector, screen, and overheads 2.1–2.4 • Chart: "Creating a Science-Rich Environment"
Preparing Your Own Environment Guide teachers as they assess their own water environments and consider ways to modify their classrooms that will stimulate water explorations.	30 minutes	
Understanding Children's Water Play Use vignettes to illustrate children's water play and the teacher's role.	30 minutes	• Overhead projector, screen, and overheads 2.5 and 2.6 • Copies of the vignette observation form, transcript to video vignette 2, and "Read and Reflect 3" • VCR, monitor, and video cued to vignette 2

Pre-assignment: Read "Getting Ready" and "Books and Web Sites," and complete the "Classroom Environment Checklist" on p. 113 of the teacher's guide. Complete the reflection questions.

Basic Workshop 2: Getting Ready

OBJECTIVES

- Gain understanding of the important elements of a science-rich learning environment
- Assess needs of own environment and plan for adaptations
- Begin to understand how children's water play is connected to science concepts and inquiry skills

OVERVIEW

- Overview of water environment (30 minutes)
- Preparing your own environment (30 minutes)
- Understanding children's water play (30 minutes)

INSTRUCTOR PREPARATION

- **PREVIEW VIGNETTE 2** and identify the points you want to make during the discussion. Refer to the following video instructions.
- **REMIND TEACHERS** to bring their "Classroom Environment Checklists."

MATERIALS

- Overhead projector, screen, and overheads 2.1–2.6
- Copies of vignette observation form, the transcript to video vignette 2, and "Read and Reflect 3"
- VCR, monitor, and video cued to vignette 2
- Chart: "Creating a Science-Rich Environment"

Activity

OVERVIEW OF WATER ENVIRONMENT (30 MINUTES)

PURPOSE: The environment is key to the children's experience. It should be stimulating and materials must be accessible. This conversation and photographs will call teachers' attention to important strategies.

1. **INTRODUCE THE TOPIC OF WATER ENVIRONMENTS** (10 minutes). Explain the importance of creating an environment that stimulates inquiry about water and motivates exploration. Creating this kind of environment means more than providing a water table; it is about selection of materials, the kind of space available, and the displays and resources that provide ideas about water exploration. Suggest that teachers review the section of the teacher's guide that talks about water environments, and give them a chance to share strategies they are thinking about. List responses on the chart you prepared, "Creating a Science-Rich Environment."

2. Discuss creating an environment that encourages exploring water (20 minutes) using overheads 2.1–2.4.

- If you have time, print the overheads on paper and place each on a piece of newsprint. Mount these around the room and ask your teachers in teams to write on each chart how this particular environment encourages inquiry. Bring teachers together and read the responses on the chart. Add important ideas to the chart you have started.

- If you are running behind schedule, use the overheads as overheads and discuss each as you project it, getting ideas about the photo from your teachers and adding important ideas that aren't mentioned.

Overhead 2.1:

How does this environment invite water exploration?

Talk about how the wire rack holds the tubes, freeing the children's hands to manipulate and pour. The tub on the floor encourages investigation of moving water up and down. Also note the display of books, materials, and posters. One of the posters lists rules for the water table and the other documents work they have been doing.

OVERHEAD 2.2:

How does this environment invite water exploration?

This photo shows a table setup. Note the use of wire racks to hold the tubes and containers at varied heights.

OVERHEAD 2.3:

How does this environment invite water exploration?

Note that a chair can also be used to provide varied heights for water movement. It can hold tubes in place and support another container for water to be moved from or into it.

OVERHEAD 2.4:

How does this environment invite water exploration?

This photo also shows a table setup; however, this one offers a challenge to move water in a cycle, up into the jug and out again into the tub.

PREPARING YOUR OWN ENVIRONMENT (30 MINUTES)

PURPOSE: An environment that encourages water exploration is carefully thought out and prepared. Assessing the strengths and needs of their own environments is the first step in preparing teachers for exploring water with their children.

1. **IDENTIFY STRENGTHS FROM THE "CLASSROOM ENVIRONMENT CHECKLIST"** (10 minutes). Ask the teachers to get out their classroom environment checklists and their reflections. Ask, "What do you have to help you create a rich environment for young water explorers?" Connect teachers' resources to the chart of ideas they have made with you. Find out if any of them have things they can share or sources others should know about.

2. **DISCUSS ENVIRONMENT NEEDS** (20 minutes). Discuss one category at a time as you review the needs they have identified and help them think about solutions. The box on the next page has suggestions for addressing each category. Before solving problems, give other teachers a chance to share their strategies, asking, "Does anyone have a suggestion for . . . ?"

Use these questions, based on the checklist, to facilitate the conversation. Focus on helping teachers with their needs.

- Do you all have enough varied materials for exploring water?
- Did anyone have issues providing space for water and displays?
- Did any of you find challenges with your schedule?
- Do you have extra adults to help?
- How are you going to find appropriate children's books?
- What concerns do you have about water spills and children getting wet?

This is an opportunity to reinforce the value of materials and time in inquiry science. Pursue these issues with a focus on solving them rather than communicating that they are not important.

- **Materials:** Water tables, tubs or containers, and materials to move, control, and contain water are essential to a successful water exploration. Allow the teachers to share what materials they have and what their issues are. If water tables are at a premium, suggest teachers borrow a table or two from another classroom for a few months. Also, cement-mixing tubs and galvanized metal tubs can act as water tables. They may also need help with preparing the water wall and pegboard. Be prepared to help them find where they are available and how to ask for what they need. If teachers are concerned about setting up the water wall or the Velcro pegboard, suggest they ask for an adult volunteer to help with the setup.

- **Space:** Water tables take up a good amount of space. Placing water tables and tubs or containers near a classroom sink is ideal but not always possible. Adding a water center to the classroom also demands space, and both the water center and the water table area get wet; therefore, there needs to be a place to store towels, mops, and sponges. Classrooms also need space for hanging up wet smocks and for storing extra sets of children's clothing. Using the space under water tables to store water play materials works well. In addition, space is needed at the children's eye level to display posters, books, pictures, or children's work. Sometimes it's necessary to rearrange a classroom temporarily and/or put some other materials away or put some furniture in storage. Some teachers move the water exploration outdoors to save classroom space and to make spilling less of an issue.

- **Time:** Children need ample time to experience the world of exploring water in a way that builds understanding. Suggest that teachers allow at least thirty to forty-five minutes of focused time to get children deeply involved in an exploration and see it through. Help teachers find ways to create blocks of time without unnecessary transitions. Remind them to allow a regular time for science talks.

- **Cleanup:** Water will undoubtedly get on the floor and children will get wet. Water smocks prevent most clothing from getting wet. Choose those that are easy to get on and off, have long sleeves, and dry fairly quickly. Prevent floors from getting too wet by covering them with either a few layers of newspaper, old towels, or rubber mats. Encourage children to keep the water in the water table and the tubs at the water center, but provide paper or cloth towels, sponges, and a mop so they can clean up spills as they happen.

- **Adults:** Although not absolutely necessary, extra adults are a big help, especially on walks. A letter to families (p. 106 in the teacher's guide) can often generate support and volunteers. Sometimes, however, volunteers are unavailable. Suggest teachers ask their administrator to help find an interested civic group, such as a local literacy organization or Chamber of Commerce.

- **Resources:** Hopefully everyone uses the library. If not, help them locate the nearest branch. You might also have them share ideas for guest experts (such as plumbers) who could supply PVC pipes and even visit the classroom.

UNDERSTANDING CHILDREN'S WATER PLAY (30 MINUTES)

PURPOSE: This activity will help teachers begin to observe their children's water play and think about who plays at the water tables and what they do. At the same time they will begin to understand the teacher's role in connecting science learning to children's ongoing dramatic and constructive play.

1. **PROVIDE AN OVERVIEW OF THE NATURE OF CHILDREN'S WATER PLAY** (10 minutes). Introduce the discussion by sharing the ideas on overhead 2.5 and 2.6. Ask for examples of children's recent water play from their classrooms as you make the following connections.

OVERHEAD 2.5: TYPES OF WATER PLAY

- **Constructive**
  Whenever children are engaged in manipulating objects to create a construction for moving water, they are engaged in constructive play. For example, some children may use tubes and T-connectors to create a lemonade stand. Other children may use tubes to create water systems that can move water in a variety of ways. We encourage this type of play by providing enough space and varied materials that fit together to make complex paths for water flow.

- **Dramatic and symbolic**
  Water play is often motivated by a story line the children are creating. Dramatic play occurs often at the water table as children pretend to cook, make magic potions, and go on boat rides. You can encourage children to focus on the science without interrupting the play by asking questions such as, "Can you add another drop to your potion?" or "Will your boat be able to take more passengers?"

- **Exploratory**
  Exploratory play describes the children's interest in exploring the properties of water with a variety of materials that help them move and contain water. As children examine a pump at work, figure out how to get water in and out of a baster, or discover strategies for getting water to move up and down through tubes, they are engaged in exploratory play.

Use overhead 2.6 to discuss some of the influences on children's play.

OVERHEAD 2.6: INFLUENCES ON WATER PLAY

- **Previous experience**
  While water is a part of all children's everyday experiences, children's experiences vary. The ideas children bring to the exploration are influenced by these experiences. Depending on the environment in which they have lived, some children may have been exposed to oceans, rivers, and waterfalls, while others have not. They may have used faucets or not paid any attention while their bath was being run. Use of books and posters can broaden children's knowledge about water and serve as an inspiration for exploring water and how it flows.

- **Culture**
  Culture also influences how children engage with the water. For example, some families may think that getting wet or "messy" is inappropriate. It will be important to help these families understand what their children gain by exploring the science of water. That is, through their water play, children will learn about important science ideas as they explore the properties of water and investigate how water moves. If children are reluctant to get wet at the water table, suggest that they work at the water center, which may seem less messy and more manageable.

- **Development**
  Children's cognitive, social, and physical development all influence their capacity to explore water. Frequent experiences with water, support for their problem solving, and encouragement with collaboration will all enhance their development in important ways.

---

2. INTRODUCE VIGNETTE 2 (20 minutes). Mention that this vignette was filmed at a Boston class for four- to five-year-olds.

    a. Distribute the transcript and the vignette observation form, and tell teachers they will use this form to take notes as they view the video, noting children's engagement and the strategies the teacher uses to encourage engagement and inquiry.

    b. Show the vignette.

    c. After the viewing, discuss observations connecting what teachers have seen to overhead 2.5: Types of Water Play. Ask the following questions:

- What types of water play did you see in this vignette?

- In what ways did the teacher encourage these types of play?

- How did she connect the play to science learning?

Look for responses like these:

- Types of play—Much of this play is exploratory. The children are using basters, tubes, and spray bottles to move water. They are experimenting with different ways to get water into the tubes, such as spraying it. There is a bit of constructive play in the placement of the tubes in the wire wall.

- Teacher encouragement—Part of this teacher's work happened before the children entered the room. She carefully selected materials that would allow the exploration of the properties of water and the ways it flows. She also put a little food coloring in the water to make it more visible as it moves through the tubes. She is sitting comfortably at the table—at the children's level—and she asks strategic questions, calling the children's attention to specific aspects of their work.

- Connection to science learning—The teacher makes important connections to the science. She gets one child to talk about the path the water will follow in the tubes and another to talk about the water in the baster—where it is when it is tipped and how to get it to come out. She keeps the conversation at the descriptive level mostly as they talk about what water is doing under different circumstances.

3. CONCLUDE THE WORKSHOP by telling teachers the concrete ways you will support them as they set up their environments. You might want to collect "Read and Reflect 2" in order to better understand their environment issues. Distribute "Read and Reflect 3," review your expectations, and confirm the time and place for the next workshop.

Basic Workshop 2: Vignette Observation Form

Name: _____

Note your observations by identifying the teacher strategies and child responses.
- Types of play the children are engaged in (such as constructive, dramatic, exploratory)
- Ways the teacher encourages exploration of water
- Ways the teacher makes connections to science concepts

Teacher Strategy	Child Response

TRANSCRIPT OF VIDEO VIGNETTE 2: FOCUSED EXPLORATION OF WATER FLOW

Scene: Three children are at the water table moving water through tubes placed in a water wall and using basters.

The children: Shakira, Dashawn, and Mikey

Teacher: How do you get the water in there?

Shakira: I try to put this—like this.

Teacher: Uh-huh.

Shakira: Then I go . . . It won't come out.

Teacher: It won't come out? How do you think you can get that out?

Shakira: If you wait for a little while . . .

Teacher: It will just pour itself out?

Shakira: If you wait for a little while, you see it get— once you've squeezed it out, and then it comes out.

Teacher: Oh!

Shakira: And then Dashawn squeeze that in there. They spray that thing in here. I'm going to try this. There.

(Children are playing without talking briefly.)

Dashawn: I'm trying to get the water inside here.

Teacher: Um-hmm.

Dashawn: And I'm trying to fill the water thing. And Mikey . . . Mikey . . . and Mikey is trying to get it to handle, but I'm pouring it *(inaudible)*.

Mikey: I'll get it.

Teacher: Oh, there it goes!

Dashawn: Now, we're trying to make the water . . .

Shakira: And I'm trying to make . . .

Dashawn: She's trying to make the water . . .

Teacher: Do you know where this ends? Where is this going? Where is this water going to go? Where is it going to go?

Shakira: Through here . . . through there.

Teacher: Uh-huh.

Shakira: And then over here.

Teacher: Yes.

Shakira: And it goes out here.

Teacher: Oh, it's going to come right up here?

Shakira: I think.

Teacher: Let's see.

Deshawn: It got a lot in, Miss Budd.

Teacher: How do you know there's a lot in there? How do you know? Because—look, I want to show you something. I don't see any water in there, so how do we know there's any in there?

Dashawn: It does go like that.

Teacher: Oh, so it's hiding up in here? Where does the water go when you turn it this way, Dashawn?

Dashawn: Watch. It's in here, and then watch this *(inaudible)*.

Teacher: I have a question, Dashawn.

Dashawn: It's right here.

Teacher: Can you get the water to come out without turning it this way?

Dashawn: Well, it will. Watch this. Watch *(inaudible)*.

Teacher: Okay. I'm watching. I'm watching. What's happening?

Dashawn: Put it this way, and then it didn't come out.

Teacher: It still doesn't come out?

Dashawn: It goes *(inaudible)*. It goes down in here.

Teacher: Does it feel like your hand is stuck—sticking to that? Let me try.

Dashawn: And see, it's down here, but sometimes it . . .

Teacher: But if you let go, it comes . . . Does it come out? Oh, look!

Mikey: That's what I'm trying to do.

Teacher: Is that what you were trying to say before?

Mikey: Yes.

Teacher: What exactly were you trying to say?

Mikey: I was saying it can't go out.

Teacher: It can't go out?

Mikey: That's right.

Teacher: It stays there.

Mikey: Uh-huh.

Teacher: Why does it do that?

Child off camera: *(Inaudible)* be squeezing?

Teacher: Dashawn. Did you see this?

Dashawn: Yes.

Teacher: Why does it come out?

Dashawn: Because it's . . . because see you have to squeeze this. You don't . . .

Teacher: You have to squeeze it to make it come out?

Dashawn: Yes.

Teacher: Otherwise it just stays there?

Dashawn: Yes. If you don't squeeze it, it does go out the tube.

Teacher: Okay.

READ AND REFLECT 3:
OPEN EXPLORATION

Name: _____

Read and Reflect

Before coming to workshop 3, read the open exploration and the science teaching sections in the teacher's guide. Respond to these questions as you reflect on what you read. This information will be helpful in the workshop discussion.

We will talk about the following two purposes of open exploration. What examples of these can you find in the open exploration steps? Be specific and note the page numbers of your reference.

1. Gives the children opportunities to wonder, notice, and explore. How exactly does open exploration do this?

2. Gives the children the support, materials, and time they need to begin their exploration. When and how does open exploration do this?

You should also answer these questions:
- How do you see involving families in these explorations? What will the benefit be to you and to the children?
- What challenges will you face as you implement open exploration for the first time?

Observe and Record

Observe children's water exploration over the course of one week and record what you see. Look for the kinds of play children are engaged in (such as constructive, dramatic, or exploratory), who is playing, and the interests being expressed. Bring this information to workshop 3.

Overview of Open Exploration

AT A GLANCE

Purpose:

- Become familiar with open exploration, its purpose, and the cycle of activity
- Gain basic understanding of the teacher's role during open exploration
- Begin to understand how children might engage in open exploration

Activity	Time: 1½ hours	Materials
Overview of Open Exploration Introduce the purpose and flow of open exploration and help teachers connect this information to their exploration from workshop 1.	45 minutes	• Overhead projector, screen, and overheads 3.1 and 3.2
Examine Young Children's Open Exploration Support teachers as they discuss their assessment of water play. Use the vignette to illustrate open exploration and its connection with children's water experiences.	45 minutes	• VCR, monitor, and video cued to vignette 3 • Copies of the vignette observation form, transcript to video vignette 3, and "Read and Reflect 4"

Pre-assignment: Read "Open Exploration," "Observation and Assessment," and "Involving Families" in the teacher's guide and complete the reflection questions. Observe children's water exploration, referring to "Read and Reflect 3" for guidance.

Basic Workshop 3: Overview of Open Exploration

OBJECTIVES

- Become familiar with open exploration, its purpose, and the cycle of activity
- Gain basic understanding of the teacher's role during open exploration
- Begin to understand how children might engage in open exploration

OVERVIEW

- Overview of open exploration (45 minutes)
- Examine young children's open exploration (45 minutes)

INSTRUCTOR PREPARATION

PREVIEW VIGNETTE 3 and identify the points you want to make during the discussion. Refer to the following video instructions.

MATERIALS

- Overhead projector, screen, and overheads 3.1 and 3.2
- VCR, monitor, and video cued to vignette 3
- Copies of vignette observation form, the transcript to video vignette 3, and "Read and Reflect 4"

Activity

OVERVIEW OF OPEN EXPLORATION (45 MINUTES)

PURPOSE: As teachers prepare to use open exploration, they will need to think about three aspects of the curriculum:

- The sequence of steps and types of experiences children will have
- The role of the teacher as a facilitator of science inquiry
- Young children's early engagement with water

1. **PROVIDE AN OVERVIEW OF OPEN EXPLORATION** (20 minutes) using overheads 3.1 and 3.2.

    a. Discuss the purpose of open exploration using overhead 3.1. Mention that teachers have engaged in an open exploration in workshop 1, making some connection to their experience as you talk.

OVERHEAD 3.1: PURPOSE OF OPEN EXPLORATION

- **Give children opportunities to wonder, notice, and explore.**
  Wondering, noticing, and exploring mark children's entry into inquiry. A carefully planned environment and teacher support are keys to open exploration. Use individual children's interests as a starting point for their engagement in dramatic or exploratory play and thus in the water exploration. Initial theories about the properties of water and the properties of objects in water can be drawn out as children talk about their water experiences.

- **Give children the support, materials, and time they need to begin their exploration.**
  Time and carefully selected materials are essential to open exploration for building the base of experience that prepares children for their later focused investigations. In these early experiences children learn about the characteristics of the materials and how they can be used to manipulate water. Teachers notice children's interests, questions, and the challenges they face as they use materials to move and contain water. This information is used to encourage engagement and focus experiences.

Ask teachers for examples of these purposes from the teacher's guide, as per the reading assignment. You might also ask what they noticed about the instructions and which features they will find especially helpful as they use the teacher's guide. Ask teachers to be specific, citing page numbers for easy reference.

This conversation is designed to help teachers learn to navigate through the teacher's guide. The ideas of those who have taken a careful look will help those who are feeling overwhelmed. Look for answers such as these:

Introduce the children to exploring water:

- In step 1 the children share previous experiences and describe things they have done with water. They use new materials to explore water, reluctant water players are encouraged, and they begin science talks—where they talk about the ways they use materials to move and hold water.

- In step 2 they are introduced to new materials and books about water, and they take a walk looking for moving water as well as continuing their exploration and science talks.

Introduce the children to appropriate ways of using the water table and the water center:

- In step 1 they plan rules for exploring water and revisit these rules after they have been used for a while.

- Rules are reinforced through conversations about the children's productive water experiences.

Children begin to engage in inquiry:

- The teacher models water play.

- In step 1 the teacher encourages children to talk about their experiences at the water table and in science talks.

- The teacher models recording, representing, and using descriptive language when talking about water experiences.

- In step 2 the teacher introduces new materials to stimulate investigations.

- A walkabout encourages the children to notice water around them and stimulates discussions about how water moves in step 2. A water vocabulary is established for use in reflective conversations.

- In step 2 the teacher uses book illustrations to build connections to children's play and encourage comparison.

- Science talks encourage reflection in step 2.

b. Present the flow of open exploration using overhead 3.2.

OVERHEAD 3.2: FLOW OF OPEN EXPLORATION

- **Step 1: Introduce children to exploring water**

  This step has three key parts:

  1. *Engage—Talk about prior water experiences and introduce the materials children will be using at the water table. This introduction sets the stage by saying this activity is important and there are particular ways to engage in it.*

  2. *Explore—Choice time provides the essential early experiences that will be continued throughout the exploration.*

  3. *Reflect—Experience sharing contributes to the classroom culture of inquiry, helping children learn to talk about their water experiences and observations, and is key to children's science learning.*

- **Step 2: Ongoing exploration and reflections**

  Introduce new materials, acknowledge water play, and encourage reluctant water players using walkabouts, and continue science talks.

Make these points as you talk about open exploration:

- The guide provides detailed instructions that teachers can follow for each step.

- All children will need a period of open exploration to become familiar with the materials and how to use them effectively.

- Open exploration will vary depending on children's prior experience and their developmental levels. Have they used different materials to move and contain water? If so, they will need less time in open exploration—some children take a week or two; others may take most of the exploration.

---

c. Emphasize the importance of sending home the family letter in the involving families section of the teacher's guide. Also, mention the assessment and observation section. Note the value of copying the observation record and using it regularly during the exploration.

2. **DISCUSS THEIR OBSERVATIONS** (15 minutes) about the types of water play and the influences on children's water play. Reinforce points made earlier during workshop 2. Ask the following questions:

   - *What kinds of water play did you see in your classrooms?*
   Encourage them to use the words *constructive, dramatic,* and *exploratory* and to give specific examples. Probe until you get enough information to understand the connections they are making.

   - *Who is playing at the water tables and who is not?*
   Be sure that teachers understand that one of their goals is to encourage everyone's engagement. Identify problems and help them find solutions.

   - *What interests are being expressed?*
   Help teachers figure out that the kinds of water play going on are the starting point for encouraging further inquiry. This early observation and sharing will set the stage for future conversations about their progress.

EXAMINE YOUNG CHILDREN'S OPEN EXPLORATION (45 MINUTES)

PURPOSE: The analysis of a video vignette will give teachers a chance to see children engaged in open exploration. Readings from the teacher's guide, teachers' own exploration, and your presentation about open exploration will take on new meaning when teachers observe children's interactions with water, the materials, and each other.

1. **DISCUSS CHILDREN'S EARLY WATER PLAY EXPERIENCES** (10 minutes). Mention that most children have a natural desire to play with water and will explore the movement of water with any material they can find. You may have an example to share or want your teachers to share observations they have about this idea. Go on to explain that it is only through many and varied experiences that children become more skilled in moving water and reflecting on their water experiences.

   Ask for teachers' observations of water play in their classrooms. Add that over time, children become better able to talk about what they are finding out about water and the materials. They will also learn which materials work best for different purposes, such as containers for holding, basters for squirting, and funnels for pouring.

2. **INTRODUCE VIGNETTE 3** (5 minutes). Explain that this vignette was filmed at the water table of a Boston Head Start. Mention that you will show the vignette twice. In the first viewing, ask teachers to focus on the types of play they are seeing and children's abilities and interests.

   a. Distribute the transcript and the vignette observation form.

   b. Show the vignette.

   c. After the viewing, discuss observations of the children's water play. Try to steer away from discussing the teacher, saving those comments for the second viewing. Ask the following questions:

   - *What types of play did you see?*

   - *What did you notice about the children's abilities and interests?*

Look for responses like these:

- Types of play—These children are engaged in exploratory play. They are using various containers to hold water and pour water from. In the process they can observe how water moves and how it looks and flows through various containers.

- Abilities and interests—The children's play reveals an interest in moving water. They are using containers, a sprinkler, a sieve, and a tube and funnel to move water around. The sprinkler and sieve provide a set of holes to pour water through. Much of the time they seem more interested in the process of moving the water than in where it is going.

- Experiences with science concepts—This play is providing experiences with the ways in which water moves and the way it looks and behaves in different containers.

3. **SHOW THE VIGNETTE AGAIN** (15 minutes). A second viewing of vignette 3 will allow teachers to focus more on their role. Remind them to take notes in the second column of the observation form. After the viewing, ask what they noticed about the teacher and the role she played. Focus them first on preparation of the environment and then on her interactions with the children.

Make these points about the teacher's approach to teaching and learning:

- Environment—The materials are carefully selected to provide varied experience with moving water.

- Encouragement—The teacher leaves the children to play on their own for part of this time. When she comes to the table, her interactions are meant to call attention to the water and how their actions are affecting it. She comments on the speed of the water and suggests that they might change the position of the tube to affect the flow of the water. She also asks where the water is going, calling the children's attention to that aspect of their play.

---

4. **CONCLUDE THE WORKSHOP** by collecting "Read and Reflect 3." Give them "Read and Reflect 4," review your expectations, and confirm the time and place for the next session.

BASIC WORKSHOP 3: VIGNETTE OBSERVATION FORM

Name: _____

VIEWING 1	VIEWING 2
Observe: • Types of play • Abilities and interests • Experiences with science concepts	Observe: • Teacher strategies

Transcript of Video Vignette 3: Open Exploration of Water

Scene: Four children are engaged in an open exploration of water at the water table.

The children: Dan-eil, Malekkie, Jottn, and Jonah

Children are quietly playing at the water table. There is some inaudible dialogue.

Dan-eil: Look what Jottn did. Look what Jottn did.

Jottn: I didn't.

Dan-eil: You did.

There is more play.

Jottn: Collette!

Malekkie: Collette!

Jottn: It's going down!

Teacher: Yes, what's going down?

Jottn: It's going inside!

Teacher: It's going inside?

Jottn: Yeah. Stop it, Dan-eil.

Teacher: Do you think the faster you put it in that it'll go down?

Jottn: Stop it, Dan-eil.

Teacher: I can see you going very fast. Why are you going so fast?

Jonah: To let it go up.

Teacher: Oh, to let it go up. See . . . if you go slow, it won't go up?

Jonah: No.

Teacher: I see Malekkie putting her hands up. Why are you putting your hands up, Malekkie?

Malekkie: So I can get the water going up.

Teacher: If you put it down, will it go up?

Jottn: We do it together. *(Inaudible.)* Aha! Aha!

Teacher: Now it's going down. Can you see that? See what's happening here? Can you watch this? Let's see where it's going.

Jottn: Inside there!

Malekkie: Collette, can you put some more paint.

Teacher: Some more *(inaudible)* color? Where do I put it?

READ AND REFLECT 4:
OBSERVING OPEN EXPLORATION

Name: _____

Make a copy of the "Observation Record" on p. 136 of *Exploring Water with Young Children*. Document observations of four or five children during an open exploration at the water table. Reflect on your observations and complete the questions below. Bring your observation record and your reflections to workshop 4.

1. What evidence do you see of children's interest in exploring water? Include specific comments and behaviors of the children.

2. What connections can you make between children's engagement and the science outcomes on pp. 120–121 of the teacher's guide? Look in the water explorer behaviors column for examples similar to those of the children.

3. What will you want to accomplish on your next exploration? What might improve the quality of children's engagement? How can you extend experiences they have had? How can you draw in new children?

4. How would you rate the quality of your observation notes? Did you record descriptive details that were useful when reflecting? What might you want to do differently next time?

Focused Exploration of Flow

AT A GLANCE

Purpose:

- Engage in a focused exploration of water's flow
- Deepen understanding of the science concepts and inquiry skills
- Experience the teacher's role as a facilitator of focused exploration

Activity	Time: 1½ hours	Materials
Discuss Observations Ask teachers to share open exploration observations briefly.	20 minutes	• "Read and Reflect 4"
Focused Exploration of Flow Facilitate a focused exploration by engaging teachers in the challenges of manipulating water's flow. Model the teacher's role by encouraging inquiry and engagement with the science concepts.	1 hour 10 minutes	• Overhead projector, screen, and overheads 1.2 and 1.3 • For each group of three or four participants: clear plastic cups or bottles with holes (three or four), additional cups or bottles without holes (optional), nail or skewer (for making holes in the bottles or cups), large plastic container, pegboard, Velcro (for the pegboard and the plastic bottles or cups with holes), water • Chart: "What We Know about Flow" • Camera and film or digital camera (optional) • Copies of "Read and Reflect 5"

Pre-assignment: Observe children's open exploration of water and complete "Read and Reflect 4."

Basic Workshop 4: Focused Exploration of Flow

OBJECTIVES

- Engage in a focused exploration of water's flow

- Deepen understanding of the science concepts and inquiry skills

- Experience the teacher's role as a facilitator of focused exploration

OVERVIEW

- Discuss classroom observations of open exploration (20 minutes)

- Focused exploration of flow (1 hour 10 minutes)

INSTRUCTOR PREPARATION

- Review "Step 3: Water in Bottles with Holes" on p. 49 of the teacher's guide. You will be modeling an exploration with elements of this process. This review will help you understand the elements of the exploration and strategies you might use for engaging teachers in inquiry.

- Gather materials you will need. Refer to p. 105 of the "Resources" section of the teacher's guide for information about purchasing and setting up these materials.

MATERIALS

- "Read and Reflect 4"

- Overhead projector, screen, and overheads 1.2 and 1.3

- For each group of three or four participants: clear plastic cups or bottles with holes (three or four), additional cups or bottles without holes (optional), nail or skewer (for making holes in the bottles or cups), large plastic container, pegboard, Velcro (for the pegboard and the plastic bottles or cups with holes), water

- Chart: "What We Know about Flow"

- Camera and film or digital camera (optional)

- Copies of "Read and Reflect 5"

Activity

DISCUSSING OBSERVATIONS (20 MINUTES)

PURPOSE: This brief conversation will give teachers a chance to share experiences and give you some information about their engagement with the material you have presented. Ideally they will continue the conversation in informal settings.

Facilitate a brief conversation in which teachers have a chance to share their early experiences with open exploration. You might ask questions like these:

- What kinds of water play are your children engaged in?

- How are children showing their interest?

- What connections have you made to the science outcomes?

- What next steps are you planning?

If issues arise and there is no time to problem solve, be sure to let teachers know how you will follow up with them.

Focused Explorations of Flow (1 hour 10 minutes)

Purpose: This experience will provide teachers with a deeper understanding of the science concepts, inquiry skills, and focused exploration—its purpose, the nature of activities, and the role that teachers play in facilitating children's inquiry.

1. **Introduce the activity** (15 minutes). Tell teachers they will be engaged in a focused exploration of water's flow, for example, as it flows out of faucets and hoses or as it pours out of containers such as bottles. Mention that the trainer will be modeling the strategies they can use to engage their children in exploration and inquiry. As with the exploration they did in workshop 1, this exploration has been designed for adults, but much of their experience can be used with children.

   Find out what teachers know about flowing water. Draw out their thoughts and observations while you list their responses on the piece of chart paper labeled "What We Know about Flow."

   Ask where they may have seen water flowing with questions such as the following:

   - Where have you seen water flowing?

   - What did the streams of flowing water look like? What influences their size? Their shape?

   - What are differences between big and little streams of flowing water?

   - What happens when a stream gets very small? Large?

2. **Begin the exploration** (10 minutes). Show teachers the materials they will be using during the first part of the activity and tell them that these materials have been chosen to help them look carefully at small amounts of water flowing. Show them the holes and point out that they are of different sizes and at different locations on the bottles. Demonstrate how the bottles can be attached, removed, and reattached to the pegboard. Remind participants that what you are doing is not exactly what they will do with children. They need to use the teacher's guide as they prepare to explore flowing water with children.

   Facilitate predictions by asking questions like, "What do you think you'll see when the bottles are filled with water?" "Will the streams of water all be the same size?" "Which ones will be bigger/smaller?" "Will they all shoot out of the bottle for the same distance and with the same force?" Discuss for a few minutes, and then let them explore with the cups or bottles in the containers with water. Encourage them to try out as many different combinations as possible. Tell them they will be asked to record some of their observations.

3. **ENCOURAGE TEACHERS' INVESTIGATION** (25 minutes). As teachers are exploring flow with these materials, walk around and observe what is going on at each group.

Pay attention to how they are exploring the materials, noticing if they are interested in the streams of water, what they seem to notice, whether they notice how the size of the holes affects how the water flows out of the cups. Do they notice that the location of the holes on the bottles affects how far the streams squirt?

As you work with each group, try modeling the teacher's role in the following ways:

- Restate the question they are investigating. ("What are you learning about the water's flow?")

- Articulate what you see them doing and add a new question to investigate. ("I see that the streams are different coming out of these two cups. What difference does the size of the hole make?")

- Encourage teachers to talk about what they notice. ("What about the holes in the bottoms? How are those streams different?" "Did you notice how small streams out of small holes break apart more quickly?")

- Revisit their predictions. ("Is that what you thought would happen?") Probe for their ideas on differences between what happened and their predictions.

- Distribute paper, pencils, and markers and ask teachers to draw the streams from different perspectives.

After about ten minutes, gather teachers together for a five-minute conversation. Begin by asking, "What did you notice about the streams coming out of different bottles or cups?" Encourage comparison of the streams coming out of different bottles and speculation about why they might be different. Draw out descriptive language about size, arc, and changes in the water flow. Wonder why and allow teachers to share their theories. Point out the value of discussions to share experiences and ideas and perhaps generate new theories. Just as it is an important part of the teachers' process, it is also important for children.

Draw one or two of the teachers' setups as a record for later conversation, or if you have a camera available, photograph some of the setups.

As teachers engage in the activity, challenge them to set up the cups or bottles on the pegboard so they can capture some of the water from one cup with another cup below. Ask them to talk about how they decided where to place the cups. Also, ask teachers to draw one or two of the interesting setups with the cups or bottles.

After about twenty-five minutes, ask teachers to stop what they are doing.

4. **DISCUSS TEACHERS' EXPERIENCES WITH THE SCIENCE CONCEPTS AND THE INQUIRY PROCESS** (20 minutes). Review overhead 1.3 (science concepts) and ask teachers to talk about the science content they experienced. Ask them questions like, "What did you notice about how the water moved with these materials. What do you think explains what was happening?"

Review overhead 1.2 (the inquiry diagram) and ask teachers what aspects of the diagram describe experiences they had during the exploration. Ask them to talk first with the group with whom they explored. Suggest that they take notes on the ideas that come up. Guide the discussion with questions like these:

- How would you describe the inquiry you just engaged in?
- Which aspects of the inquiry diagram did you experience during your exploration?

After about ten minutes, bring teachers together to talk in a large group. Ask first about inquiry. Let one group start and have others add ideas not mentioned. Ask questions such as these:

- Did identifying questions play a role in your exploration of water's flow? What role did it play?
- How did the predictions you made influence your investigation?
- What data did you collect? How did you collect it? How did you use it?
- What role did collaboration and sharing across groups play in your investigating and thinking?
- When and how did you draw some conclusions about the cause of the variations in the flow coming from the cups?

Refer back to the experience they just had and discuss how you might begin such an experience with young children. If they have trouble coming up with ideas, suggest they begin by talking about times the children might have experienced water flowing (such as with a hose or from a faucet). They would want to encourage some description of the water's flow. They might also show the materials to be used and ask the children to predict what might happen during the exploration.

5. **CONCLUDE THE WORKSHOP** by collecting "Read and Reflect 4." Give them "Read and Reflect 5," review your expectations, and confirm the time and place for the next workshop.

READ AND REFLECT 5:
FOCUSED EXPLORATION

Name: _____

Before coming to workshop 5, read the focused exploration and extensions in the teacher's guide. Observe a small group of children (two to four) engaged in exploring water and complete an observation record (p. 116 in the teacher's guide). Respond to these questions as you reflect on what you read and observe. This information will be helpful in the workshop discussion.

In workshop 5 we will talk about the purposes of focused exploration. What examples of these can you find in the steps of focused exploration?

1. Help children gain deeper understandings of exploring water. How exactly does focused exploration do this? What teaching strategies (refer to the teacher's role in "Resources") are key?

2. Encourage continued use of the water environment. When and how does focused exploration do this?

3. What challenges will you face as you implement focused exploration for the first time?

4. What science concepts were the children working on (water movement, water taking the shape of its container)? Describe specifically what you saw and heard as evidence of each concept you mention.

5. What inquiry skills were being used? Be specific about what you saw and heard.

Overview of Focused Exploration

AT A GLANCE

Purpose:

- Become familiar with focused exploration, its purpose and sequence
- Gain basic understanding of the teacher's role during focused exploration
- Continue to build understanding of the science concepts and inquiry skills and how they are expressed in children's behaviors and conversation
- Begin to understand what children's focused exploration might look like
- Build deeper understanding of the difference between open exploration and focused exploration, as well as the transition between the two

Activity	Time: 1½ hours	Materials
Discuss Observations Facilitate a conversation in which teachers share their classroom experiences.	30 minutes	• "Read and Reflect 5" • Overhead projector, screen, and overheads 1.2 and 1.3
A Closer Look at Focused Exploration Give teachers an overview of focused exploration, its purpose and flow. Connect their exploration of flow to this content. Use a vignette to illustrate what focused exploration looks like in a classroom.	1 hour	• Overhead projector, screen, and overheads 5.1–5.3 • VCR, monitor, and video cued to vignette 2 • Copies of transcript to vignette 2 (in basic workshop 2), vignette observation form 5, and "Read and Reflect 6"

Pre-assignment: Read focused exploration and extensions. Conduct an observation and respond to reflection questions.

Basic Workshop 5: Overview of Focused Exploration

OBJECTIVES

- Become familiar with focused exploration, its purpose and sequence
- Gain basic understanding of the teacher's role during focused exploration
- Continue to build understanding of the science concepts and inquiry skills and how they are expressed in children's behaviors and conversation
- Begin to understand what children's focused exploration might look like
- Build deeper understanding of the difference between open exploration and focused exploration, as well as the transition between the two

OVERVIEW

- Discuss observations (30 minutes)
- A closer look at focused exploration (1 hour)

INSTRUCTOR PREPARATION

- Preview video vignette 2. Prepare for using the video vignette by previewing it and identifying the key points you want to make about these children and the way the teacher focuses their experiences with water. If you would like to develop your understanding of focused exploration or that of the teachers, vignettes 4, 5, and 6 also illustrate aspects of focused exploration.

MATERIALS

- VCR, monitor, and video cued to vignette 2
- Overhead projector, screen, and overheads 1.2, 1.3, and 5.1–5.3
- Copies of the transcript to video vignette 2 (in basic workshop 2), vignette observation form 5, and "Read and Reflect 6"

Activity

DISCUSS OBSERVATIONS (30 MINUTES)

PURPOSE: Provide another opportunity for sharing experiences, addressing issues that have surfaced, and encouraging collaboration between teachers.

Facilitate sharing classroom experiences using these questions to guide the conversation: (You might want to show overheads 1.2: "Inquiry Diagram" and 1.3: "Science Concepts" during this conversation.)

- What inquiry skills have children been using? (Probe for specific evidence to support their statements.)

- What science concepts are your children exploring?

- How do you plan to encourage further inquiry and promote deeper science understandings? (Spend some time helping them think about how to use the teacher's guide and which next steps are appropriate.)

> You might want to collect and review teachers' observations and reflections. You will get a sense of how well they understand the workshop content. You will also get ideas for follow-up.

A CLOSER LOOK AT FOCUSED EXPLORATION (1 HOUR)

PURPOSE: This interactive activity will familiarize teachers with focused exploration, its purpose and flow. They will gain a deeper understanding of young children's inquiry and what it looks like in the classroom. A vignette showing a teacher and children exploring water is used to illustrate what focused exploration looks like in a classroom.

1. PROVIDE OVERVIEW OF FOCUSED EXPLORATION USING THREE OVERHEADS. (Take no more than 30 minutes for this.) Refer teachers to the focused exploration section of the teacher's guide. Tell them that you are going to help them understand the purpose and flow of activity, their role as a teacher, and what children's focused exploration might look like.

a. Introduce focused exploration by reviewing overhead 5.1.

OVERHEAD 5.1: PURPOSE OF FOCUSED EXPLORATION

- **Give children opportunities to investigate specific questions in depth**
  The term "focused" refers to the investigation of a particular question or idea about water. The term "investigation" implies that the children are deepening their use of inquiry through prediction, planning, data collection, and analysis. Children's understandings grow as they pursue their own particular interests and questions.

- **Give children the support, materials, and time they need to deepen their exploration**
  Whether in open or focused exploration, time, materials, and support are always key to inquiry-based science. Remember that the teacher's role as a guide is key when it is time to engage in the more advanced skills of inquiry like data collection and analysis.

Help teachers make connections to their experiences in the last exploration by asking, "What specific activities did you engage in during the first exploration of water that would exemplify focused exploration?" Question further by asking, "How was that different from the open portion of the exploration?" Teachers may also want to talk about their exploration of flow.

b. Show overhead 5.2 and review the elements of focused exploration for exploring water and flow. Refer the teachers to p. 13 in the "Getting Ready" section of the teacher's guide during this conversation.

OVERHEAD 5.2: ELEMENTS OF FOCUSED EXPLORATION

- **Exploration focuses on water flow, drops, and sinking and floating**
  In order to experience and think about the various properties of water more deeply, children need opportunities to explore it in many ways. Focused play with materials such as containers, tubes, funnels, and containers with holes gives children experience with the ways water moves and takes the shape of containers, which leads to a closer look at how water in the form of drops focuses on adhesion and cohesion. Also, sinking and floating activities raise questions about objects in water. The focused exploration section of the teacher's guide provides detailed descriptions for each of these investigations.

- **School and neighborhood walkabouts heighten awareness of water in everyday life**
  Children experience water repeatedly in their everyday lives. They can watch water coming out of the faucet in the bathtub and they may even have toys they play with in the water. They see rain coming down, landing on the window, the ground, and dripping off of the eaves on their house. Helping them make connections between these experiences and their exploration of water in the classroom leads to a heightened awareness and capacity to examine the properties of water in these varied settings. These extensions, either around the school or neighborhood, are a part of focused exploration for this purpose.

- **Books and visiting experts stimulate exploration and thinking**
  Children's motivation and ideas about their work are fueled by seeing water in various settings and the ways water is represented by illustrators, learning about the roles of people associated with water movement and seeing the tools of their work (such as plumbers).

- **Two- and three-dimensional representation as well as movement supports reflection on work**
  The process of drawing or creating a three-dimensional representation refocuses children on what they have done, encourages close examination, and offers new challenges as they change medium.

- **Science talks allow for sharing experiences, ideas, and formulating new theories**
  Regular conversations provide opportunities to share water experiences and theories about why water is flowing in particular ways. Children learn from each other and bring new insight into their next water experiences.

c. Use overhead 5.3 to discuss the transition from open to focused exploration. (Refer them to p. 34 in the teacher's guide.) Connect these points back to comments they made when discussing their observations. Help them understand who in their classrooms is showing signs of being ready to focus.

OVERHEAD 5.3: THE TRANSITION FROM OPEN TO FOCUSED

Look for children who:

- **Spend a full choice time playing with water**
  You may see children choosing the water table at the beginning of choice time and remaining there. They may connect their play from one day to the next by making a lemonade stand repeatedly, or just enjoy pouring water from one container to another.

- **Become deliberate in how they move water**
  For example, as children watch the flow of water through a tube and move the tube to speed up or slow down the water.

- **Choose to explore water regularly**
  Do you see the same children at the water table or other water centers day after day?

Connect these ideas to those on overhead 5.1 by sharing that these children are engaged in inquiry by exploring important ideas about the properties of water in a more focused way. They may be closely examining the way it flows down or strategies for moving it up or sideways. Their exploration and emerging questions reflect the beginning of investigation. They are already focused on water as an activity—now is the time to focus them on deeper explorations.

2. **VIEW AND DISCUSS VIGNETTE 2** (20 minutes). Introduce the vignette by saying that it is the same vignette they watched in workshop 2. It was taped at a Boston class for four- and five-year-olds and shows three children playing at the water table. Explain to teachers that they will view the vignette twice.

   a. Before the first viewing, distribute the transcript. Tell teachers to note the children's engagement and learning as they watch the vignette. Show the vignette and then let them share their comments for a few minutes. You might refer them to the teacher guide chart of outcomes and review it before starting the video.

   b. Prepare them for the second viewing of the video by giving each teacher a copy of the vignette observation form. Ask them to examine the role the teacher plays this time and note their observations in the teacher column of the form. They can also note additional observations about the children.

   c. Show the video and give them a few minutes to record observations and thoughts.

   d. Bring groups together and guide a discussion using the following questions:

      • Why would you characterize this vignette as a focused exploration? (Probe for specific examples.)

      • This teacher played a key role in the children's experience. What did she do to encourage engagement and guide inquiry?

      • What might the next step be for these children?

You might want to highlight the following points when discussing vignette 2.

Look for ideas like these about the children's engagement and focused exploration:

- These children are engaged in exploring focused questions. ("How can I get the water to move through this tube?" "How does water behave in this baster?") The teacher asks Shakira to predict the path of the water through the tube she has placed in the wire wall. Many of their descriptive comments are a form of data. They are describing the behavior of the water. As they work, new questions emerge. (For example, "Why doesn't the water come out of the baster when it is turned upside down?") As children discover what water looks like in different containers, how it flows in tubes, from sprayers, and from basters, they are learning about the properties of water.

- These children are focused on specific aspects of water—moving it through tubes, getting it into and out of basters. They are able to describe what they are doing and seeing.

Look for ideas about the role the teacher plays:

- The teacher is an enthusiastic observer of the children's actions, is attending to what interests them, and is encouraging them to articulate what they are doing and thinking. The teacher plays an important role in the children's inquiry with the questions she asks. She uses questions to focus the children's observations. ("How do you get the water in there?") She asks for predictions. ("How do you think you can get it out?" "Where is this water going?") She also poses challenges. ("Can you get the water to come out without turning it this way?")

- Further examination of any of these questions would be good next steps. The teacher could return to Shakira to talk about how the water actually did flow through the tube. Was it as she predicted? Were there any problems getting the water to flow up? Did she figure out a way to do that? This could be documented with drawings and Shakira's descriptions. If she had problems they could be brought to the group for discussion with the generation of possible solutions.

- The teacher might also encourage the boys to document the water in the baster in different positions. There are questions to pursue here as well. ("Why doesn't the water come out of the baster when it is turned tip down?" "How can you get the water out if you are holding it sideways?") She might come back to these on another day at the beginning of choice time, reminding children of this experience and posing one of these questions again.

3. **In conclusion,** refer teachers again to "The Teacher's Role," p. 97 in "Resources" in the teacher's guide. They will find further description of strategies to use during focused exploration here. Collect "Read and Reflect 5" and distribute "Read and Reflect 6." Remind teachers of the time and place for the next workshop.

Basic Workshop 5: Vignette Observation Form

Name: _____

Viewing 1	Viewing 2
Observe:	Observe:
• Types of play	• Teacher strategies
• Abilities and interests	
• Experiences with science concepts	

READ AND REFLECT 6:
OBSERVING FOCUSED EXPLORATION

Name: _____

Observe a small group of children (two to four) engaged in focused exploration, and complete an observation record (p. 116 in the teacher's guide). Respond to these questions as you reflect on what you observed.

1. What characterizes this activity as focused exploration?

2. What science inquiry skills were the children using? Refer to the science outcomes chart in the teacher's guide and make specific connections between the skills listed and children's comments and behaviors.

3. What science concepts were the children exploring? Refer to the outcomes chart and make specific connections between the concepts listed and your children's comments and behaviors.

4. What might be appropriate next steps for these children? Please explain how each idea will encourage further inquiry and promote deeper science understandings. Refer to specific steps in the teacher's guide.

5. How would you rate the quality of your observation notes? Did you record descriptive details that were useful when reflecting? What might you want to do differently next time?

Focused Exploration of Drops

AT A GLANCE

Purpose:

- Engage in a focused exploration of drops
- Deepen understanding of the science concepts and inquiry skills
- Extend understanding of the teacher's role as a facilitator of focused exploration

Activity	Time: 1½ hours	Materials
Discuss Observation Facilitate a brief exchange of teachers' observations from focused exploration.	20 minutes	• "Read and Reflect 6"
Focused Exploration of Drops Facilitate an exploration of drops with an emphasis on noticing variations in size, shape, and movement on different surfaces. Model the teacher's role by encouraging inquiry and engagement with the science concepts.	1 hour 10 minutes	• Chart: "What We Know about Drops" • Overhead projector, screen, and overhead 1.3 • For each group of three or four participants: water, food coloring (optional), eyedroppers, Plexiglas or rigid plastic plates, wax paper, and at least three other papers and materials as surfaces for drops (such as aluminum foil, paper towels, construction paper, fabric scraps) • Reference books with pictures of drops • Paper, pencils, and markers • Camera and film or digital camera (optional)

Pre-assignment: Complete "Read and Reflect 6," conducting an observation and responding to the reflection questions.

Basic Workshop 6: Focused Exploration of Drops

OBJECTIVES

- Engage in a focused exploration of drops
- Deepen understanding of the science concepts and inquiry skills
- Extend understanding of the teacher's role as a facilitator of focused exploration

OVERVIEW

- Discuss observation of focused exploration (20 minutes)
- Focused exploration of drops (1 hour 10 minutes)

INSTRUCTOR PREPARATION

- Review "Focused Exploration: Drops" in the teacher's guide. With this step from the teacher's guide fresh in you mind, you can make valuable connections to what participants will be doing with children.
- Gather the necessary materials. Refer to p. 105 in the "Resources" section of the teacher's guide for information about purchasing and setting up these materials.

MATERIALS

- "Read and Reflect 6"
- Chart: "What We Know about Drops"
- Overhead projector, screen, and overhead 1.3
- For each group of three or four participants: water, food coloring (optional, but makes drops more visible), eyedroppers, Plexiglas or rigid plastic plates, wax paper, and at least three other papers and materials as surfaces for drops (such as aluminum foil, paper towels, construction paper, fabric scraps)
- Paper, pencils, and markers (use for drawing drops)
- Camera and film or digital camera (optional)
- Copies of "Read and Reflect 7"

Activity

DISCUSSING OBSERVATION (20 MINUTES)

PURPOSE: As teachers share their experiences, you will have a chance to encourage collaboration and ongoing dialogue about science teaching. You will also be able to identify issues that need addressing.

Facilitate a conversation in which teachers share their recent experiences with focused exploration. You might use questions like these:

- What inquiry skills have your children been using? (Ask for specific evidence to support their statements.)

- What science concepts are your children exploring? (Again, ask for specifics.)

- How do you plan to encourage further inquiry and promote deeper science understandings? (Spend some time helping them think about this. Use the teacher's guide as a reference.)

- What kinds of dramatic play (if at all) do your children engage in when they are playing with water? How can this play be connected with the science?

> You might want to collect and review participants' observation and reflection sheets. They will give you a sense of how well teachers are understanding the workshop content and suggest ideas for follow-up.

FOCUSED EXPLORATION OF DROPS (1 HOUR 10 MINUTES)

PURPOSE: This activity will help the teachers deepen their understanding of focused exploration as it applies to drops and the teacher's role during focused exploration. In addition, they will deepen their science understandings.

1. **INTRODUCE THE ACTIVITY** (15 minutes). Tell teachers that in this session they will continue to explore the properties of water. Similar in format to workshop 4, this session will engage them in a focused exploration of drops.

   Find out what teachers know about small amounts of water, particularly drops. Ask where they have seen drops and gather descriptive information by asking what they have noticed about the drops they have seen. Call attention to specific characteristics such as size and shape. Ask for some comparison of drops in different circumstances. List their responses on the chart labeled "What We Know about Drops."

2. **BEGIN THE EXPLORATION** (10 minutes). Show the participants the eyedroppers and Plexiglas and ask, "What do you think you'll see when you put drops on the Plexiglas?" Ask questions that focus teachers on ideas about size, shape, and movement: "How big do you think the drops will be?" "Will they all be the same shape?" Encourage teachers to suggest ideas they might try out.

   Distribute eyedroppers and Plexiglas to groups of three or four and encourage teachers to find out all they can about drops on Plexiglas. Ask them to pay attention, in particular, to the shapes of the drops, and to observe from the side as well as from above.

   If teachers seem to have difficulty focusing, call their attention to the drops with techniques like these:

   - Restate the question they are investigating. ("What can you learn about drops?")

   - Articulate what you see them doing and add a new question to investigate. ("I see you are making lots of little drops. How can you make them bigger?")

   - Encourage teachers to talk about what they notice, keeping the focus on the shapes of drops and how drops can (or cannot) be moved with the droppers (such as blowing gently or tilting the Plexiglas).

- Revisit teachers' predictions and probe for differences between predictions and outcomes.

- Distribute paper and pencils and ask teachers to draw drops from different perspectives.

Gather teachers together for a conversation. Ask, "What did you notice about drops as you put them on Plexiglas and other surfaces?" Encourage teachers to show what they are describing with the materials and (where appropriate) the drawings they made. Focus teachers on the shapes and movement of the drops.

3. **ENCOURAGE TEACHERS' INVESTIGATION** (25 minutes). Extend the investigation by passing out at least three different kinds of paper to each group. Ask for predictions on how drops will differ on these various papers and from those on Plexiglas. Ask them to think about what qualities of paper will account for differences. Allow at least ten minutes for this investigation.

   Bring teachers together to talk about drops. Encourage comparison of drops as they appear on different surfaces. Draw out descriptive language about size, shape, and patterns of movement. Wonder why and allow teachers to share their theories. Point out the value of discussions to share experiences and ideas and perhaps generate new theories.

4. **FACILITATE A DEBRIEFING** (10 minutes). Gather participants together and ask them to talk about the science content they experienced. Review overhead 1.3 (science concepts). As teachers talk about observations and experiences and encourage them to show what they are describing.

Properties of Water: Cohesion and Adhesion

Water molecules stick together *(cohesion)*. When the amount is small, cohesion causes water to form drops. It also causes *surface tension* as a "skin" forms at water's surface. Some bugs, for example, can scoot across the surface of a pond, and a glass of water can be slightly overfilled without spilling.

Water sticks to other materials *(adhesion)*. It sticks more or less strongly depending on the material. Water does not stick to wax paper, so drops remain round, but it sticks to paper towels or newspapers, so drops are pulled apart.

Ask for experiences with cohesion. Talk about shape as visible evidence that water is pulled together. Then ask the same questions about adhesion.

5. **REVIEW THE TEACHER'S ROLE** (10 minutes). Ask the teachers to reflect on the role you have been playing. Guide their conversation with the following questions:

   - How has this exploration provided experiences with the science concepts?

   - I have been leading you through an investigation of drops. What have I been doing and why do you think I chose to do those things? (Probe for specifics about the role you played and the rationale for your comments, questions, and the instructions you gave.)

   - How does this relate to the role you will play with your children? (Encourage teachers to talk about strategies that they can use and whether they are just as you did it or if they have reasons to make modifications.)

6. **IN CONCLUSION**, collect "Read and Reflect 6" and distribute "Read and Reflect 7." Remind teachers of the time and place for the next workshop.

READ AND REFLECT 7:
REVISIT SINKING AND FLOATING

Name: _____

Reread the sinking and floating section of the teacher's guide. As you reflect on what you read, consider how the *Exploring Water with Young Children* approach to sinking and floating is similar or different from what you have done with children in the past. Record your thoughts about these similarities and differences on the following questions. Be as specific as you can.

1. How is the approach to inquiry and science concepts similar or different?

2. How is the role of the teacher similar or different?

3. What are the strengths of each approach?

4. What are the challenges of each approach?

Focused Exploration of Sinking and Floating

AT A GLANCE

Purpose:

- Engage in experiences that help participants think about some elements that contribute to whether an object sinks or floats, and confront the commonly held misconception that "heavy things sink, and light ones float"
- Engage in inquiry
- Build capacity to draw science learning from experience
- Recognize that engaging children in sink and float experiences helps to develop skills of inquiry and expands their experiences with sinking and floating

Activity	Time: 1½ hours	Materials
Facilitate investigation of sinking and floating Engage teachers in an investigation of sinking and floating that includes placing objects in water and making clay boats.	1 hour	• Clear plastic bucket for each group of 4–6 people • Water • Variety of common objects for sinking and floating (such as a rock, pencil or other piece of wood, button, and so on) • Enough balls of plasticine so that each participant has one about 1½–2 inches in diameter • About 100 small weights (such as metal washers, pennies, or marbles) to use as "passengers" for boats • Paper towels
Discuss young children's exploration of sinking and floating Discuss what children actually gain from investigations of sinking and floating and view a video vignette of children engaged in such an investigation.	30 minutes	• VCR, monitor, and video cued to vignette 4 • Copies of "Basic Workshop Evaluation" for each teacher

Pre-assignment: Reread the sink and float section of focused exploration in the teacher's guide.

Basic Workshop 7: Focused Exploration of Sinking and Floating

OBJECTIVES

- Engage in experiences that help participants think about some elements that contribute to whether an object sinks or floats, and confront the commonly held misconception that "heavy things sink, and light ones float"

- Engage in inquiry

- Build capacity to draw science learning from experience

- Recognize that engaging children in sink and float experiences helps to develop skills of inquiry and expands their experiences with sinking and floating

OVERVIEW

- Facilitate investigation of sinking and floating (1 hour)

- Discuss young children's exploration of sinking and floating (30 minutes)

INSTRUCTOR PREPARATION

- Gather materials you will need for the sink and float investigation.

- Preview video vignette 4. As you preview the video, consider how it exemplifies the points you want to make about children's sink and float investigations.

MATERIALS

- Clear plastic bucket for each group of 4–6 people

- Water

- Variety of common objects for sinking and floating (such as a rock, pencil or other piece of wood, button, and so on)

- Enough balls of plasticine so that each participant has one about 1½–2 inches in diameter

- About 100 small weights (such as metal washers, pennies, or marbles) to use as "cargo" for boats

- Paper towels

- VCR, monitor, and video cued to vignette 4

- Copies of "Basic Workshop Evaluation" for each teacher

Activity

Facilitate Investigation of Sinking and Floating (1 hour)

Purpose: This experience with sinking and floating is designed to build understanding of teachers' understanding of how and why things sink and float, and continue to enrich their understanding of inquiry.

1. **Introduce the investigation** (15 minutes) by asking teachers what they know or think they know about sinking and floating. List responses on a board or chart paper. Ask for their reasons or an example to support what they said.

> Encourage a conversation by asking the teachers to say what they think, regardless of whether they are certain about being "correct." Many adults do not fully understand this concept and may have naïve conceptions, such as "Heavy things sink." Having such a view is fine for now, reflecting limited experience and/or limited reflections on experiences.

2. **Begin the investigation** (15 minutes) in a large group. Have a large, clear bucket filled with water, and a few objects in a place visible to all. Ask teachers to describe each of the objects in as many ways as they can (including size, shape, weight, and the materials out of which it is made). Ask them to predict whether each object will sink or float—and why they think so. Make sure they talk about why they think so before the objects are put into the water. Encourage the group to begin to think about the relationships between the characteristics of the object and whether the object will sink or float.

Ask different teachers to place each object in the water one by one. Have the group observe and record what happens and discuss the results. Were their predictions accurate? Were there any surprises? Encourage the group to raise questions, wonder, and speculate about what they have seen.

Begin the work with plasticine by asking teachers to try one of the small pieces to see whether it will sink or float. Ask teachers whether they think it will sink or float. As people make their predictions, be sure to ask them why they think so. Then put the plasticine in the water. Once all have observed it sink, ask, "Is there any way you might be able to make this plasticine float?"

3. **Begin work in small groups** (15 minutes) by sending teachers to other buckets around the room with enough plasticine for everyone. The challenge is to find ways to make the plasticine float. As you visit groups, encourage them to discuss what they need to do to make the plasticine float, and to share what seems to be working and what does not. Help them focus on what seems to be working by asking whether one boat sank as quickly as another. Encourage them to notice what happened—where the water came in and which shapes seem most promising. These questions can help them realize that even objects that sink, sink differently based on some of their characteristics. Remind teachers to dry the plasticine after they put it in water.

Ask teachers to do some sketching of their clay boats, drawing two pictures of unsuccessful boat designs, and two successful ones. Try to accurately reflect where the water line is in relationship to the boat. As individuals or groups have some success, challenge them to test out cargo (such as pennies, marbles, or washers) to see how many each particular boat can carry.

This exploration with clay will expose participants to these processes of inquiry:

- Plan, predict, and take action
- Observe closely
- Collect, record, and represent experiences
- Gather data

4. **FACILITATE A DEBRIEFING** (15 minutes). Bring the teachers together and ask them about the ways they got the clay to float. Encourage them to talk about the process they used to change the clay. For example, someone might say they made the clay into a boat shape. Ask, "What parts of the boat were you focusing on?" "What seemed to make a difference?" Encourage people with different kinds of designs to talk about their success. Also, ask what did not seem to work, and whether people now might consider why those designs did not work.

Then ask, "So what did we find out about factors that affect whether something will sink or float?" In this case the focus has been on changing the shape of the clay. In other words, things don't necessarily sink if they are heavy; it depends on their shape.

Make a point of mentioning that this conversation has supported teachers' inquiry by engaging them in reflection on their experience (exploring patterns and relationships and constructing reasonable explanations) and encouraging them to ask new questions.

DISCUSS YOUNG CHILDREN'S EXPLORATION OF SINKING AND FLOATING (30 MINUTES)

1. **TALK ABOUT WHAT CHILDREN GAIN FROM A SINK AND FLOAT INVESTIGATION** (10 minutes). Start by asking teachers who have engaged children with sinking and floating to share what they hoped their children would gain from the experiences they provided. Many teachers include an experience with sinking and floating in their teaching. While sinking and floating is a phenomenon clearly within children's daily experience, it is often not made clear just why it is included in early childhood programs. Their responses are likely to include some version of process skills, such as "trial and error," or "critical thinking." Their responses might also include something about the science content, such as "to understand what makes things float." Remind teachers that the experience they have just had certainly engaged them in inquiry and using science process skills, as they talked about earlier. Remind them also that the science concepts of density and buoyancy are difficult to understand, and beyond young children's understanding. The purposes of engaging children in sinking and floating experiences include the following:

- Engage children in inquiry
- Encourage children to observe and describe objects in water, discovering that some sink, some float, some stay suspended, and others sink or float depending on their shape (what's inside them, what they are made of, or if something is holding them up)

Remind participants that children will not be able to explain sinking and floating based on these experiences, but that these experiences are valuable for developing skills of inquiry, extending their skills, and will be the basis for a later understanding of density and buoyancy.

2. VIEW VIGNETTE 4 (20 minutes). Introduce video vignette 4, which shows an investigation of sinking and floating in a Connecticut preschool classroom. The children are using rigid tubes filled with water and small objects made of different materials. Ask teachers to note the similarities and differences between their exploration and the children's.

Show the vignette and use the teachers' comments as a starting point for talking about exploring sinking and floating with children. Use the following questions and possible responses to guide the discussion:

- *"In what ways was this exploration similar to the one you just engaged in?"*
  While there were many differences in these two explorations, they followed a similar format. They began with a review of prior experiences and ideas about sinking and floating, spent some time making predictions about what would sink and what would float, continued with exploration designed to provide new data, and concluded with a science talk that reviewed the data and included the sharing of ideas about why things sink or float.

- *"How was this exploration different from yours?"*
  The exploration the teachers just participated in covered more ground (objects in water and making clay boats) and addressed the science in more depth, both in the experience and the discussion. This is an important distinction for the teachers to understand. The exploration and processing will take more time for young children, and each step in the exploration process will need repeating before moving on to one that is more complex. On the other hand, there are things the teacher in the vignette could do to help the children get more out of the exploration at this point in time.

- *"What could this teacher do to help the children engage more fully with the science they are experiencing?"*
  There are two main points to make here. First, she might have used a different recording system. The chart with children's drawings provided a meaningful opportunity for data collection, but she might have also charted their predictions to use as a reference. More important, she might have focused the children on the characteristics of the objects they were working with and used this as a way to talk about what sank and what floated. Conversation and documentation about these characteristics will further children's thinking and can be used to deepen their ideas over time as they add new experiences to this one. It also can lead to new questions for investigation.

3. IN CONCLUSION, distribute the basic workshop evaluation and have your teachers complete it, if time allows, or arrange to collect it later. Let the teachers know how you will be following up and supporting their implementation of the teacher's guide.

Suggested Next Steps

- This is an ideal time to start a mentoring program. Teachers will be enthusiastic about using the teacher's guide, but they will also have some clear ideas about the challenges.

- You might also want to start the advanced workshops soon. Give teachers a month or so to work with additional workshops based on their expressed needs.

- You might also want to intersperse the workshops with guided discussions. Use the guidance on p. 198 as you plan. Guided discussions provide an opportunity for teachers to share their successes and challenges as they try new approaches to teaching science.

Transcript of Video Vignette 4: Exploring Sinking and Floating

Scene: A teacher and a small group of children are investigating sinking and floating. In the first scene, the teacher introduces the investigation to the whole group. In scene 2, they carry out the investigation and talk about what they found.

Scene 1

Teacher: I would just like to talk a little about this. Does anybody remember doing this?

Children: Me! Me!

Teacher: Becky, can you tell me a little bit about what happened when you used the different materials? What you did with the tube?

Becky: I put it down and the water went up and down, and the toy stuff was coming down.

Teacher: So, some things came down or did everything come down?

Becky: Not everything.

Child: Only one thing.

Teacher: The bear stayed up?

Becky: Yeah, the bear stayed up and the other stuff went down.

Teacher: How did it go down? Did it go right down or did some of them go down?

Child: It wasn't that heavy.

Becky: Because it wasn't that heavy and it went down to the bottom.

Teacher: So, if it wasn't that heavy, how did it go down if it wasn't that heavy? How did it go down the tube?

Becky: It went slowly down.

Teacher: And if it was heavy what happened?

Becky: It wouldn't go down.

Teacher: If it was heavy it didn't go down?

Becky: *(Shakes head no.)*

Teacher: Like if you put a marble in there, what would the marble do? Do you remember what the marble did?

Becky: Just go down.

Teacher: It just went down.

Becky: Went quickly down and then the tube went sideways and the toys went down.

Teacher: Oh, so you did it sideways too? You held your tube sideways?

Becky: It went in the middle. It stayed in the middle.

Teacher: What stayed in the middle? What stayed in the middle?

Becky: All of them.

Teacher: All of them stayed in the middle when you held it sideways? I have a challenge for you. We have some materials and some tubes and I would like to see if you could make one tube with the materials that you think are going to float and one tube to put the materials in that you think are going to sink.

Scene 2

Becky: I think this is going to go down.

Teacher: The marble. You think the marble's going to go down?

Becky: Yeah.

Teacher: Can you tell me why you think it's going to go down?

Becky: This is going to float.

Teacher: Going to float. Can you tell me why the marble is going to go all the way down?

Becky: Cause it's hard.

Teacher: It's hard. Hmm. You got any ideas, Danielle?

Becky: This going to stay on top.

Nick: Maybe the hard ones go on top and the little ones go down to the bottom.

Teacher: Maybe the hard ones . . .

Nick: Go up to the top and the little ones go down to the bottom.

Teacher: You think? Hey, Nick. Would you like to fill your tube?

Nick: Sure.

Teacher: What do you think that one's going to do?

Danielle: Float down.

Teacher: You think it's going to float down. Fast or slow?

Danielle: Fast.

Teacher: Can you ask your friends what they think?

Danielle: *(No response.)*

Teacher: Want to ask your friends what they think?

Danielle: *(Shakes head no.)*

Teacher: Becky, Lindy, and Nick. Nick. Danielle thinks that's going to go down the tube fast. What do you think?

Michael: I think it's going to sink.

Teacher: That did go fast. Do you have any ideas why that went fast? I wonder why that went fast. See if you hold them like this . . . like this . . . good.

Nick: Have you noticed how that part of the water goes up?

Teacher: Yeah. Wow. What is that? What's doing that?

Becky: I think it's going to go down fast.

Danielle: Yeah.

Teacher: Let's see if we can guess . . .

Child: Look at, Miss Linda—they roll back and forth.

Teacher: You've got a lot of marbles in there.

Child: I've got four in there. A black one, a blue one, a red one, and a green.

Teacher: My question would be what makes something float? Think about that just for a . . .

Nick: Pressure.

Teacher: Pressure. That's a good answer. Pressure. Can you tell me a little about that? Is there a reason why you told me pressure?

Nick: I don't know.

Teacher: Pressure—was that pressure inside the tube?

Nick: Pressure inside.

Teacher: Pressure from the water or pressure from the object?

Nick: Pressure from the object.

Teacher: Oh, very good observation. Becky . . .

Becky: It float on the top.

Teacher: Do you know why? Do you have ideas why?

Becky: The water was making it go up and the pumpkin stayed up on top, because it was light.

Teacher: It was light. That's a good idea. So the pumpkin stayed up on top so the water . . . it was the water that it was floating on?

Becky: And the marbles went down.

Teacher: Do you have any ideas as to why the marbles went down the way they did?

Becky: Because some was going up and some went down because there *(inaudible)* up and down.

Teacher: Oh.

Becky: And that went down . . . I shaked it up. It went down.

Teacher: When you shaked it up that went down . . . like when . . . shake it up as in turned it?

Becky: It went down.

Teacher: That's interesting.

Becky: It went down.

Teacher: Thank you, Becky.

Teacher: You think it is going to go down fast? What was that?

Becky: A marble.

Teacher: A marble. Try something that you think might go down slow or float. You can put it right in there—we're just going to keep it in there, then we can compare them.

Becky: That floats, Miss Linda!

Teacher: It does float. What is that? What did you put in there?

Becky: It's a stick and that floats too.

Teacher: Why don't you put the cover on, Becky, and then switch it back and forth and see what it does?

Lindy: This floats. This floats.

Teacher: That does. Yes, it does.

Lindy: Look at the dolphin one.

Teacher: See what happens?

Danielle: It's not going. It's not going.

Teacher: It's not going. How come?

Danielle: Don't know.

Teacher: Good job, Lindy.

Teacher: 'Cause that's a floater. Do you want to try something else?

BASIC WORKSHOP EVALUATION

Name (optional): _____

1. To what degree have the workshops
   helped you learn about these topics:

   The science of exploring water

   ☐————☐————☐————☐————☐
   not at all　　　*adequate*　　　*significant*

   Science teaching

   ☐————☐————☐————☐————☐
   not at all　　　*adequate*　　　*significant*

   Using the teacher's guide

   ☐————☐————☐————☐————☐
   not at all　　　*adequate*　　　*significant*

2. Overall, I found the level of challenge to be:

   ☐————☐————☐————☐————☐
   not at all　　　*challenging*　　　*much too*
   challenging　　　　　　　　　　*challenging*

   Please explain:

3. Overall, I found the workshops to be valuable
   to my science teaching:

   ☐————☐————☐————☐————☐
   not at all　　　*valuable*　　　*extremely*
   valuable　　　　　　　　　　*valuable*

   Please explain:

4. To what extent have you already applied
   learning from the workshops to your work?

   ☐————☐————☐————☐————☐
   no　　　*some*　　　*extensive*
   application　　*application*　　*application*

   Please describe one approach that has had
   the greatest effect on children's learning:

5. What new insights have you gained about teaching an inquiry-based science curriculum? Please explain your answer (be specific):

6. What new insights have you gained about *your role* in relation to young children's science learning?

7. What do you suggest we do differently next time?

EXPLORING WATER WITH YOUNG CHILDREN
GUIDING PRINCIPLES

- All three- to five-year-olds can successfully experience rich, in-depth, scientific inquiry.

- The science content draws from children's experiences, is interesting and engaging, and can be explored directly and deeply over time.

- Expectations are developmentally appropriate; that is, they are realistic and can be tailored to the strengths, interests, and needs of individual children.

- Discussion, expression, and representation are critical ways in which children reflect on and develop theories from their active work.

- Children learn from one another.

- Teachers take on specific roles to actively support and guide children's science learning.

INQUIRY

Engage, notice, wonder, question

Focus observations, clarify questions

Plan, predict,
take action

Ask new
questions

Explore, investigate

Observe
closely

Reflect on experience,
explore patterns and
relationships, construct
reasonable explanations

Collect, record, represent
experiences and data

**Share, discuss, and reflect with group;
draw conclusions; formulate ideas
and theories**

Science Concepts

- Water flows

- Water takes the shape of its container

- Cohesion

- Adhesion

- Objects can sink, float, or stay suspended in water

- Air takes up space and floats to the top of water

How does this environment invite water exploration?

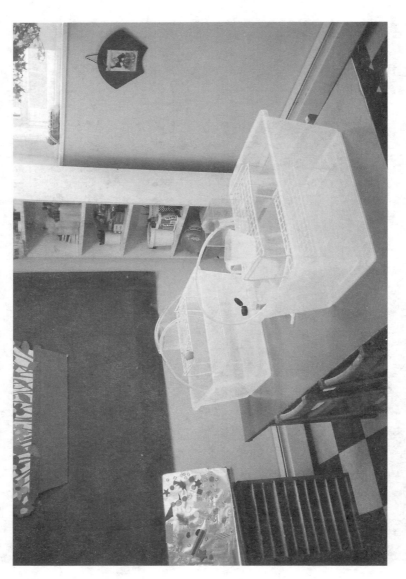

How does this environment invite water exploration?

How does this environment invite water exploration?

How does this environment invite water exploration?

Types of Water Play

- Constructive

- Dramatic and symbolic

- Exploratory

INFLUENCE ON WATER PLAY

- Previous experience

- Culture

- Development

PURPOSE OF OPEN EXPLORATION

- Give children opportunities to wonder, notice, and explore.

- Give children the support, materials, and time they need to begin their exploration.

Flow of Open Exploration

- Step 1: Introduce children to exploring water

- Step 2: Ongoing exploration and reflections

PURPOSE OF FOCUSED EXPLORATION

- Give children opportunities to investigate specific questions in depth

- Give children the support, materials, and time they need to deepen their exploration

ELEMENTS OF FOCUSED EXPLORATION

- Exploration focuses on water flow, drops, and sinking and floating

- School and neighborhood walkabouts heighten awareness of water in everyday life

- Books and visiting experts stimulate exploration and thinking

- Two- and three-dimensional representation as well as movement supports reflection on work

- Science talks allow for sharing experiences, ideas, and formulating new theories

THE TRANSITION FROM OPEN TO FOCUSED

Look for children who:

- Spend a full choice time playing with water

- Become deliberate in how they move water

- Choose to explore water regularly

advanced workshops

Overview

The eight advanced workshops are designed to build teachers' ability to engage children in scientific inquiry. Although the workshops are numbered, they are in no particular order. However, you may want to start with workshop 8: "Creating a Culture of Inquiry about Exploring Water." In this workshop, teachers assess their skills as science teachers. The results can help you create a sequence of workshops that responds to the interests and needs of teachers. All of the ninety-minute workshops use an instructional approach that encourages application of new ideas. The presentation of new material is combined with activities that encourage teachers to apply what they are learning as they analyze classroom practice and children's work, and as they plan the next steps.

The advanced workshops include the following:

8. **CREATING A CULTURE OF INQUIRY ABOUT EXPLORING WATER:** This workshop addresses the environment and climate of a classroom that encourage exploration of water and its properties, including strategies for conveying the excitement, challenge, and wonder that can occur when children investigate water flow, drops, and sink and float. Teachers complete an evaluation of their skills as science teachers and develop individual goals for professional development.

9. **DEEPENING CHILDREN'S SCIENCE UNDERSTANDINGS:** This workshop addresses the ways teachers can deepen children's science understandings by encouraging and guiding their inquiry.

10. **USING BOOKS TO EXTEND SCIENCE LEARNING:** This workshop helps teachers integrate books into their ongoing science exploration. The role, selection, and use of fiction and nonfiction books in an investigation of water will be covered.

11. **ASSESSING CHILDREN'S SCIENCE LEARNING:** This workshop addresses the critical role of assessment as teachers discuss young children's science learning—the outcomes they might expect, how to document engagement and learning, and how they can use their documentation to plan next steps.

12. **ENCOURAGING REPRESENTATION:** This workshop addresses the importance of representation. Strategies for encouraging children to use movement and varied art media to communicate their observations and understandings are discussed.

13. **USING CHILDREN'S REPRESENTATIONS AS TEACHING TOOLS:** This workshop draws on knowledge and skills built in workshop 12, "Encouraging Representation," by helping teachers use children's work to deepen their science understanding.

14. **FACILITATING SCIENCE TALKS:** This workshop addresses what is often considered the most difficult aspect of science teaching—facilitating successful large group and small group science talks.

15. **MAKING AND USING DOCUMENTATION PANELS:** This workshop takes teachers through the process of making panels and addresses how these panels can be used as a springboard for stimulating discussions, reenactments, and further exploration.

ASSIGNMENTS

Each advanced workshop has a pre-assignment. Pre-assignments include readings in the teacher's guide; reflection questions; and gathering materials, such as children's work, to discuss in the workshop. These assignments prepare teachers for participating fully in workshop discussions and activities. Be sure to distribute them at least one week before the workshop, emphasizing their importance.

ADVANCED WORKSHOP INSTRUCTIONS

The instructions for each workshop follow the same format as the basic workshops. Each workshop includes the following sections:

- At a Glance outlines the purpose, activities, timeline, materials, and pre-assignment for each session

- Objectives identify what skills you want teachers to gain by the end of the session

- An overview describes the activities and how much time to devote to each one

- Instructor Preparation lists the materials you need and how to prepare for each session

- Detailed step-by-step instructions provide guidance for leading each activity

- Handouts to copy for each participant

- Overheads to copy as transparencies before each session

- "Read and Reflect" pre-assignments to copy and distribute at least a week before each workshop

Handouts, overheads, or assignments appear after most workshop instructions. You will also find suggested next steps, which offers ideas that help teachers with follow-up, as they apply their new learnings to their classrooms.

"Next Steps" include the following:

- Strategy handouts: In many workshops, teachers develop lists of strategies they have found useful, read about in the teacher's guide, or seen in vignettes. Type up strategies and distribute them.

- Plan another workshop: Choose one that builds on the skills teachers are developing. Be sure that teachers have time to work with the content of at least one workshop before offering another. We suggest one-month intervals.

- Plan guided conversations: Focused conversations in small groups are an excellent way for teachers to deepen their understandings and build their ability, once the content has been presented. Help teachers create relevant documents from their classrooms to use as material that stimulates thought and discussion. For example, videotaped or audiotaped science talks would make excellent documents for discussion after workshop 14. Transcribing is a great idea as well.

- Mentoring: Individual support may be the best way to support teachers. Careful examination of teachers' work supports reflective practice, while giving you the insights needed to tailor your approach based on teachers' interests and needs.

- Recommended reading: The bibliography is full of valuable books and articles. Distribute these to teachers at strategic points during the workshop. Be sure to use this material to build your understanding of science teaching and learning as well.

Creating a Culture of Inquiry about Exploring Water

AT A GLANCE

Purpose:
- Build strategies for creating a culture of inquiry
- Assess knowledge and skills as science teachers
- Set goals for professional development as science teachers

Activity	Time: 1½ hours	Materials
Define term "culture of inquiry" Present characteristics of a culture of inquiry and use a video vignette to illustrate your points.	40 minutes	• Chart: "Strategies for Creating a Culture of Inquiry" • VCR, monitor, and video cued to vignette 1 • Overhead projector, screen, and overhead 8.1
Complete self-assessment Engage teachers in completing the "Evaluating Science Teaching" form (p. 206). Facilitate small group discussion of needs and goals.	35 minutes	• Copies of "Evaluating Science Teaching"
Conduct collective goal setting Have groups share their goals and issues, and make plans for supporting further professional development.	15 minutes	• Copies of small group recording form • Charts: "Our Strengths as Science Teachers" and "Our Needs as Science Teachers"

Pre-assignment: Read the introduction to the teacher's guide.

Advanced Workshop 8: Creating a Culture of Inquiry about Exploring Water

OBJECTIVES

- Build strategies for creating a culture of inquiry about water
- Assess knowledge and skills as science teachers
- Set goals for your own classroom

OVERVIEW

- Define term "culture of inquiry" (40 minutes)
- Complete self-assessment (35 minutes)
- Conduct collective goal setting (15 minutes)

INSTRUCTOR PREPARATION

- **ASSIGN READING.** At least one week before the workshop, ask teachers to read the introduction to the *Exploring Water with Young Children* teacher's guide.

- **CONSIDER OBSERVING TEACHERS IN THE CLASSROOM AT THIS TIME.** This will give you valuable information about teachers' science teaching. Start by deciding which parts of the "Evaluating Science Teaching" form you want to use. If the teachers are beginners, it might not be appropriate for them to use the whole form. As teachers become more skilled, you will want to expand the aspects of their practice that you are focusing on. Use the following when planning your observations:

    - When evaluating beginning teachers, focus on sections I A, B, and C; section II A1 and A2, and B1.

    - When evaluating developing teachers, focus on the sections that you used for the beginning teacher and add section I D and the rest of section II.

    - When evaluating teachers who are refining their skills, use the whole form.

- **PREVIEW VIGNETTE 1.** Look at the vignette, being sure that you understand the points that should be made.

MATERIALS

- Three charts: "Strategies for Creating a Culture of Inquiry," "Our Strengths as Science Teachers," and "Our Needs as Science Teachers"
- VCR, monitor, and video cued to vignette 1
- Overhead projector, screen, and overhead 8.1
- Copies of evaluating science teaching (p. 206 in the resources section) and small group recording forms (one for each group)

Activity

DEFINE TERM "CULTURE OF INQUIRY" (40 MINUTES)

PURPOSE: To build a common understanding of the elements that contribute to a positive and productive climate for science learning.

1. **INTRODUCE THE WORKSHOP AND THE TERM "CULTURE OF INQUIRY"** (10 minutes). Give a quick overview of the workshop. Explain that one of the most important roles inquiry-based science teachers will play is to create a "culture of inquiry about water exploration." This culture promotes children's investigation of water and its properties. In this environment, the physical space and the interactions with materials and people convey the excitement and wonder of exploring water. Review overhead 8.1, providing a quick overview of the elements of this culture. You will discuss them more in-depth after viewing the vignette.

OVERHEAD 8.1: THE CULTURE OF INQUIRY

- **An emphasis on the importance of exploring water**
  A water environment conveys the importance of exploring water in various ways. It emphasizes use of many kinds of materials that allow children to move and contain water, and the excitement of using inquiry to learn about the properties of water. The importance of this exploration is conveyed through provision of time and space, selection and display of varied materials, and displays that stimulate interest and reflect children's recent experiences with water and their ideas.

- **An emphasis on inquiry**
  Water explorers ask questions, observe closely over time, and think about what their observations tell them. The teacher's role is not to provide the answers, but to encourage the children to ask questions and support them as they seek answers. There is an emphasis on gathering data (or evidence) and recording it for reflection and analysis. The room is filled with children's work, photographs, charts, and panels that communicate the value of documentation.

- **Sharing observations and experiences**
  In a culture of inquiry, children are encouraged to share their experiences and ideas through small and large group science talks, and they learn to listen to what others have to say. They share their records of what they have done or their ideas about science concepts, such as how to make water flow from one container to another or how to make it flow faster. They learn that all ideas are valued, that people have different ideas, and that one can learn by asking questions of others.

- **Recording observations and experiences**
  Water explorers spend a great deal of time recording what they do—using careful sketches and descriptive words to most accurately remember their experiences. They use their records to reflect with others and find patterns in their explorations. Water explorers use a variety of other media to represent their actions and ideas, including movement and demonstration.

---

2. **USE VIGNETTE 1 TO ILLUSTRATE THESE POINTS** (30 minutes). Introduce the vignette, saying that they will be viewing the vignette they saw in basic workshop 1 again. Ask them to note the specific environmental and interaction strategies the teachers are using to create a culture of inquiry about water.

   Show the vignette and then ask for comments. Project overhead 8.1 while you talk. Guide teachers to identify specific strategies and note them on your chart. Connect each to the characteristic (from overhead 8.1) to which the strategy relates. Be sure their ideas include both environment and interaction strategies.

Look for ideas like these:

- Materials used for exploring water were carefully selected to help children experience the properties of water.

- Teachers showed the importance of water exploration by sitting at the water table or center, worked with the children, and conversed with them about what they were doing.

- Teachers' questions focused the children and helped them collect and analyze the details of their work.

- Teachers encouraged reflection on ideas and experiences.

- Various media were used to help children represent and communicate their experiences, data, and ideas.

COMPLETE THE SELF-ASSESSMENT (35 MINUTES)

PURPOSE: While these key strategies are fresh in the teachers' minds, it will be important to help them think about the ones they need to build into their repertoire. This process will help you determine the content and form of professional development that will be most helpful to teachers right now.

1. **DISTRIBUTE "EVALUATING SCIENCE TEACHING"** to each teacher and ask them to take the next fifteen minutes to complete it. Emphasize the importance of openness. Remind the teachers that they all have strengths and weaknesses as teachers, but probably most are willing to acknowledge that science teaching is not a strength. The teachers' ability to examine their own work will be the first step toward building the kind of reflective practice that will support their development as science teachers.

   While they work, move around the room, seeing that everyone is on task. Help them interpret items that might confuse them.

2. **AFTER FIFTEEN MINUTES, ASK TEACHERS TO WORK IN SMALL GROUPS,** synthesizing their evaluation information (20 minutes). Help teachers divide into groups of three or four and give each group a "Small Group Synthesis Form." Review the questions. Ask them to have a conversation and note their thoughts on the form as they talk. Suggest they have a note taker as well as someone who facilitates the conversation, ensuring they address all of the questions in the allotted time.

CONDUCT COLLECTIVE GOAL SETTING (15 MINUTES)

PURPOSE: This is an opportunity for you to collect some "data." Where do these teachers see their strengths and needs? Your responsiveness to their needs and interests will generate enthusiasm.

1. **BEGIN THE CONVERSATION BY FOCUSING ON THEIR STRENGTHS** (5 minutes). Quickly let each group share their thinking. In any group, the strengths and needs will vary from teacher to teacher, but look for themes, as well as for teachers who can support others in particular areas. Note their thoughts on the chart you prepared. You will want to refer to this information later.

2. **NOW GATHER THEIR THOUGHTS ABOUT THEIR NEEDS** (10 minutes). Repeat the process. Be sure each group has a chance to share. If you have time, encourage them to think about the next steps. You might want to offer alternatives, such as attending workshops, participating in guided discussions, and mentoring.

Suggested Next Steps

- Make a handout of the strategies teachers listed and distribute it.

- Offer workshops that best address the teachers' needs and interests.

- Design guided discussions that best address the teachers' needs and interests.

- Meet with each teacher individually to go over their evaluation, set goals, and make professional development plans. See the mentoring section for suggestions. We recommend that you conduct an observation in each room and fill out your own evaluation form before meeting with individual teachers.

- Suggested reading from the references:

"Creating an Environment for Science in the Classroom," chapter 2 in *Doing What Scientists Do: Children Learn to Investigate Their World,* by E. Doris (Heinemann, 1991).

SMALL GROUP SYNTHESIS FORM

As a group, share your individual thoughts about your strengths and needs, and record them below. Note where there was common agreement and where there was a lot of difference.

Our strengths as science teachers include:

Our needs as science teachers include:

Areas we would like to develop first:

Deepening Children's Science Understandings

AT A GLANCE

Purpose:
- Build understanding of the strategies teachers can use to deepen science understandings as children engage in inquiry
- Apply these strategies to design next steps for the teacher featured in the video vignette
- Deepen understanding of water and its properties

Activity	Time: 1½ hours	Materials
Provide overview of how young children learn science Provide a rationale for this teaching approach by discussing how young children learn science.	20 minutes	• Overhead projector, screen, and overheads 9.1–9.4
Identify strategies for deepening children's science understandings Use excerpts from a teacher's journal to identify strategies for deepening children's science understandings.	20 minutes	• Chart: "Strategies for Deepening Children's Science Understandings"
Facilitate exploration of bubbles Facilitate a brief exploration of the science the children are experiencing in the vignette that will be used in the next activity. Help the teachers understand that interaction of air and water is producing these bubbles.	20 minutes	• For each group: turkey baster, piece of clear flexible tubing (approximately 2 feet long and that fits snugly on the baster), small tub of water, cup or other container (for pouring water)
Analyze a vignette Ask teachers to analyze the strategies used by the teacher in the video vignette. In small groups, ask teachers to develop the next steps the teacher might take.	30 minutes	• Overhead 1.2 • VCR, monitor, and video cued to vignette 5 • Copies of transcript of vignette 5 and vignette observation form

Pre-assignment: Read "The Teacher's Role" in resources (see p. 97) and "Lemonade Stand: Excerpts from a Teacher's Journal" (see p. 10), both in the teacher's guide. Complete reflection questions.

Advanced Workshop 9:
Deepening Children's Science Understandings

OBJECTIVES

- Build understanding of the strategies teachers can use to deepen science understandings as children engage in inquiry
- Apply these strategies and design next steps for the teacher featured in the video vignette
- Deepen understanding of water and its properties

OVERVIEW

- Provide overview of how young children learn science (20 minutes)
- Identify strategies for deepening children's science understandings (20 minutes)
- Facilitate exploration of bubbles (20 minutes)
- Analyze a video vignette (30 minutes)

INSTRUCTOR PREPARATION

- **ASSIGN "READ AND REFLECT."** Distribute "Read and Reflect 9" at least one week before the workshop.
- **PREVIEW VIGNETTE 5.** Watch the vignette, and understand how it illustrates the points you want to make.

MATERIALS

- Overhead projector, screen, and overheads 1.2 and 9.1–9.4
- VCR, monitor, and video cued to vignette 5
- Copies of transcript to vignette 5, vignette observation form, and "Read and Reflect 9"
- Chart: "Strategies for Deepening Children's Science Understandings," with two sections ("Encourage Exploration" and "Deepen Science Understanding")

Activity

OVERVIEW OF HOW YOUNG CHILDREN LEARN SCIENCE (20 MINUTES)

PURPOSE: To set the stage for the content that follows, building the connection between inquiry and its role in science learning with what we know about how young children learn.

1. **INTRODUCE THE WORKSHOP** and provide a quick overview of the main goals of an inquiry-based teacher (5 minutes). After introducing the topic of the workshop, show overhead 9.1: "The Science Teacher's Goals." Emphasize that the focus here is inquiry science and

that this workshop will focus on the second and third goals—how teachers can guide children's inquiry and deepen children's science understandings. Mention that this might seem obvious, but in practice it is very difficult and these workshops are all designed to help them accomplish these goals.

Overhead 9.1: The Science Teacher's Goals

- **Encourage children to explore water**
- **Guide children's inquiry**
- **Deepen children's science understanding**

---

2. **Provide overview of how children learn science** (20 minutes) using overhead 9.2. Make the point that the inquiry approach to teaching science is based on what we know about the nature of science, as well as what we know about how children learn. Use the references to excerpts from a teacher's journal to illustrate the points, or ask teachers if they can make these connections.

Overhead 9.2: Science Teaching and Learning

- **Young children develop ideas about science from their life experiences**
  In the April 12 and 20 entries, the teacher asks questions that focus the children's attention and engages them in thinking about what the water is doing and why. This beginning exploration of cause and effect results in early theories about the properties of water and how it moves and looks in various containers.

- **New experiences lead children to challenge previous naïve ideas**
  In the April 20 entry, the children are exploring conservation, a concept about which young children usually have naïve theories. In the May 15 entry, Lynne refers to magic; however, by May 18 she understands that Gabi did something to adjust the speed of the water.

- **A balance between exploration and thinking, reasoning, and theorizing provides a strong basis for learning**
  The excerpts from a teacher's journal provide a picture of how this balance plays out over time. Repeated patterns of doing and talking can deepen children's understanding over time. The May 15 through June 1 entries are an excellent example of interaction between doing and talking.

- **Inquiry that leads to science learning takes time**
  These journal entries provide a good example of the kind of time it takes for children to build new understandings through inquiry. The quality of the children's inquiry deepens with time. For example, the question about the speed of water flow on May 15 was more complex than the pouring on April 12 when they weren't even paying attention to where the water went. By June 1, the children are articulating their own questions. Children gradually learn to use inquiry, becoming an integral aspect of their learning process.

- **With guidance, children have the ability to engage in all aspects of the inquiry process**
  In these journal entries, the teacher uses her observations of the children's play to pose questions for consideration and investigation (see May 15 and 18). Her documentation of children's explorations and ideas helped them extend their investigations from one day to the next, and deepen the inquiry and learning over time. Teacher follow-up provided the structure needed to help children plan, carry out, and report on an investigation. The May 15 to 22 entries illustrate this.

---

3. CONCLUDE BY MAKING KEY POINTS ABOUT THIS APPROACH (5 minutes). Use overheads 9.3 and 9.4 to focus your comments.

OVERHEAD 9.3: KEY IDEAS ABOUT THIS APPROACH TO SCIENCE LEARNING

- **Building understanding of important science concepts is an appropriate goal for young children**
  The vignettes and children's work samples included in workshops 1 through 6 and the teacher's guide illustrate young children's capabilities in science.

- **Children naturally form ideas about the world based on their life experiences**
  When exploring water, children's ideas are often revealed through the ways they manipulate the materials in order to move water. Careful observation of their efforts will give you important ideas about what they think will work and what they are trying to do.

- **In inquiry-based science it is important for teachers to provide new experiences that can lead children to more sophisticated theories**
  Our goal is to provide new experiences that will contribute to the development of new, more reasoned understandings. In particular, we hope children will begin to use evidence (what they have observed) as they build their ideas of how the world works. Comments, questions, and challenges that reflect our understandings of what they are trying to accomplish as they use materials to manipulate water are helpful in this process.

OVERHEAD 9.4:

"Experience is not the best teacher. It sounds like heresy, but when you think about it, it's reflection on experience that makes it educational."

George Forman
Professor Emeritus, University of Massachusetts

As teachers view overhead 9.4, explain that you will help them think about their role in providing the right experiences, helping children focus on the science in those experiences, and guiding a meaningful reflection process.

IDENTIFY STRATEGIES FOR DEEPENING CHILDREN'S SCIENCE UNDERSTANDINGS (20 MINUTES)

PURPOSE: The analysis of excerpts from a teacher's journal will highlight strategies teachers can use to promote children's science understandings.

1. ANALYZE EXCERPTS FROM A TEACHER'S JOURNAL TO IDENTIFY STRATEGIES (15 minutes). Ask teachers for strategies they found in the journal entries, noting their responses on the chart you have prepared. Use the question about literacy and math to highlight where science provides opportunities to promote learning early literacy and math concepts. Ask for specifics about what the journal says and connect it to the strategy they have identified.

An important point: deeper understandings grow out of reflection, but they are only possible with carefully focused experiences that happen over time. Look for strategies like these:

Encourage children's exploration:

- Used comments and questions to focus the children on the flow of water (April 12)
- Used her observations of their activity and a question about how they were adjusting the speed of the water to focus their investigation on an important question about water flow (May 15)
- Provides different-shaped containers based on her observations of their play (April 20)
- Documented children's play to help them extend the experience (May 15)
- Supporting children's dramatic play (such as with the lemonade stand) as a way to engage them in science (May 22)

Deepen children's science understandings:

- Repeatedly used her documentation of children's experiences and ideas to stimulate discussion about the science (May 15, 18, and 22)
- Careful observation of the questions and interests revealed in the children's play was a key strategy this teacher used to focus the children on particular science concepts, as well as engage them in thinking about cause and effect and develop ideas about why water moved in particular ways
- Made an intentional effort to improve children's engagement and participation in science talks; shortening the time and using concrete materials helped the children focus and communicate their actions and ideas

Supported literacy and math development:

- Repeatedly modeled the purpose and value of print with her documentation (The use of children's words in print is a powerful way to introduce the connection between the written and spoken word and interest children in learning to use print.)
- The children were given many opportunities to develop their language, which allowed for learning and using new vocabulary and communicating their experiences, observations, and ideas.
- Math was used several times in the process of collecting and recording data. On April 12, children measured how far the water squirted. On May 4, they used a measuring cup to find out how much water the jug would hold. On May 11, they used counting to keep a record of how many funnels and connectors they used in their lemonade stand.

Facilitate Exploration of Bubbles (20 minutes)

Purpose: This brief but essential experience will give teachers the science background they need to engage in a discussion of the vignette in the next activity.

1. **Introduce the exploration** (5 minutes). Tell teachers that they will be watching a video vignette of children engaged in water play. They will take a few minutes to experience what the children and teacher encountered.

   Use an empty baster and piece of tubing to demonstrate how the groups will be setting up the experience. Place the tubing on the end of the baster. Hold the empty end of tubing up, with the baster bulb side down, below. Tell teachers that the children poured water into the empty end of the tubing. Ask the teachers what they think will happen when they pour water into the open end of the tubing.

2. **FACILITATE THE EXPLORATION** (10 minutes). Ask groups to assemble their tubes and basters, and to try this out with water for a few minutes. As they do so, spend a few moments with each group to ask them to describe what they are experiencing. In the vignette, children notice that when the tube is filled with water, bubbles rise from the bottom to the top of the tubing, and pop when they reach the surface of the water. If the teachers do not see any bubbles, encourage them to try squeezing the bulb of the baster. Remember that this is meant as a very brief experience. Be certain that each group has observed the bubbles before asking them to stop.

3. **CONDUCT DEBRIEFING** (5 minutes). Ask teachers what they think caused the bubbles to behave as they did. As they recognize that air is coming out of the tube and baster, talk about the science. In particular, mention how air takes up space and was in the tube and baster before the water. As the water comes up it pushes out the air that floats to the top. Remind them that children are not likely to understand the relationship between air and water as they explore this phenomenon. Rather, this is a first experience that is likely to support their later understanding.

ANALYZE VIDEO VIGNETTE (30 MINUTES)

PURPOSE: Analyzing classroom practice will help teachers make the transition from theory to practice. While the vignette shows one point in time, in your discussion with the teachers you can put these isolated events into a context of inquiry that will build over the course of days and weeks.

1. **REVIEW THE STRATEGIES LISTED ON THE POSTER** (5 minutes). Ask teachers if they have anything to add after reading the section on the teacher's role. Add their specific strategies to the list. Suggest that they can look for these strategies in the vignette, as well as add new ones.

2. **USE VIGNETTE 5 TO FURTHER DISCUSS HOW TO DEEPEN SCIENCE UNDERSTANDINGS** (15 minutes). Begin by noting that this vignette was filmed at a Boston kindergarten. Distribute the vignette observation form and suggest teachers take notes, observing the children's behavior and the strategies used by the teacher in the vignette.

As you discuss their observations, put new strategies in the appropriate column on the chart, either "Encourage Exploration" or "Deepen Science Understanding."

Look for ideas about the science such as:

- The children are working with basters and tubes. They are investigating the ways they can get water into these materials, what water looks and behaves like in the tubes and basters, and how to get it out again. As they examine the bubbles they are beginning to learn about how air behaves in water.

Look for strategies that encourage use of inquiry such as:

- Encouraging close observation (The teacher asks the children to describe what they are doing and seeing. She asks them to demonstrate in order to observe more closely.)

- Encouraging reasoning (The teacher asks if this is the same phenomena that Rodney talked about. While the children are not providing theories about what is happening, their understanding can be revealed in other ways such as the request to contrast two observations.)

- Predicting or challenging ("What if you don't make bubbles, will it still spray?")

Note the teacher's enthusiasm and curiosity—the way she builds on what the children are doing and probes for the meaning that can be drawn out of their actions and observations. She effectively acknowledges the collaboration that went on among the children.

3. **DISCUSS THE NEXT STEPS THE TEACHER MIGHT MAKE TO EXPAND THE CHILDREN'S INQUIRY** (10 minutes). Put the inquiry diagram on the overhead projector (overhead 1.2). Point to the circle that illustrates the cyclical nature of inquiry in focused exploration, saying you want them to think about this aspect of inquiry as they plan strategies for deepening children's science understanding. Use the following questions to guide a discussion:

- What were children's interests and questions?

   – The children were interested in the flow of water into and out of the basters and tubes and the ways the bubbles were produced in this process.

- How might the teacher use inquiry to deepen understanding about one or more of these science concepts? (You might pick one to focus on, then move on to another if there is time.)

   – One child is exploring the impact of putting pressure on the water in a baster. They are noticing air in water—air taking up space, air floating up, and water moving down unless pushed up. These encounters with bubbles are accidental and not yet predictable to children.

- What next steps might the teacher take to extend this experience?

   – Documenting the children's experiences with bubbles would be a good first step. This might be done with descriptive dictation, photographs, or children's drawings. The process of dictating or drawing will lead to further investigation if they begin to wonder what the bubbles looked like, whether their appearance changes as they move through the water, and what exactly happens when they reach the top of the water. The documents can be used to remind children of these discoveries and as stimulus for helping them plan new investigations of bubbles.

   – With these documents they could begin a chart about when and where they see bubbles. Collecting this data in one place will prepare children to eventually analyze this data, developing some generalizations about when bubbles appear and some initial thoughts about why.

– Another line of inquiry might be about basters, and the impact of squeezing the bulb. While water generally moves down, basters are a great way to begin looking at how water can be made to move up.

Emphasize that deepening children's science understandings can't happen in one day, but takes place over a week or two. Remind your teachers of the importance of documentation so they can build on children's experiences from one day to the next. For example, use children's representations of water flow or your photographs as a springboard for discussion, focusing on placement of tubes and effect on the movement of the water.

In closing, encourage teachers to continue sharing what they are doing in their classrooms. Remind them when and where the next workshop or guided discussion is and what they need to do to prepare.

Suggested Next Steps

• Make a handout of the strategies teachers have listed and distribute it.

• Follow up with teachers. Ask if they have any issues with focused exploration or with their role as a facilitator of inquiry. You might ask, "What are children's current interests and questions? How do they show these?" Do teachers find ways to help children collect and record their data and talk about what it means?

• Offer the workshops on science talks or on representation as a way of extending the conversation about inquiry and deepening understanding.

• Guide a few discussions on these concepts. Film video vignettes in teachers' rooms to use for discussion. Help them consider next steps and plan ways to support how children collect and analyze data.

• Suggest readings from the references:

Cooperative Problem Solving in the Classroom: Enhancing Young Children's Cognitive Development, by Jonathan Trudge and David Caruso (NAEYC, 1988).

Using Photographs to Support Children's Science Inquiry, by Cynthia Hoisington (NAEYC, 2002).

Transcript of Video Vignette 5:
Making Bubbles

Scene: Four children (only three who speak in this vignette) are at the water table with their teacher. In the course of their play with basters and tubes they discover ways to produce bubbles. They work to recreate what one of the children has done.

The children: Ronnie, Linda, and Denisha

Linda: I'm trying a different way.

Teacher: You're trying a different way? What are you doing?

Linda: I'm trying to . . . I stuck this base thing . . .

Denisha: Oh, *(inaudible)* that, Linda. That's pretty neat.

Ronnie: I did it. I was like this . . .

Denisha: Linda, would you do this?

Teacher: Okay. We've got to make sure that the baster is pointing down into the water.

Denisha: Okay. I want to try what Linda's doing. That looks pretty nice.

Teacher: Okay, so—so, you go under and you make bubbles first? Is that what you do?

Ronnie: Yes.

Teacher: So, you make the bubbles.

Ronnie: You do this.

Teacher: You squeeze it under water, and make bubbles, and then what?

Ronnie: You do this. You can make bubbles under water.

Teacher: Oh, and it sprays water. Well, what happens if you don't squeeze and make bubbles? Will it still spray? What if you don't make the bubbles?

Ronnie: It won't spray.

Teacher: Yes. Don't make the bubbles.

Ronnie: It won't spray.

Teacher: It won't spray? May I try?

Denisha: Oh, Linda, your idea was right!

Teacher: So, I'm putting it in the water.

Denisha: It filled up!

Teacher: You're right. It doesn't spray. It's not as *(fast)*. I was sitting here—

Denisha: What Linda said was right, because when I put water in, I start going all the way back up.

Teacher: What do you mean?

Denisha: To the tubes.

Teacher: I missed the idea.

Denisha: Because see, when Linda was doing—see, Linda was like this—see, she started going back up, and her idea was right. It was going back up.

Teacher: So, what did you do, Linda, exactly? What do you do first? Maybe we could try that too. What do you do first?

Linda: First you take this . . .

Teacher: So, first take the *(baster)* . . .

Linda: Of this—dump all the water out.

Teacher: Okay. Everybody dump the water out. You want to all try it?

Linda: You take the—this.

Teacher: Take the *(baster)*.

Linda: And you slip it into the *(tube)*.

Teacher: Okay. Now, wait—we didn't all get a tube yet.

Linda: Slip it into the tube.

Teacher: Okay. Slip it into the tube.

Linda: And then—

Denisha: But I didn't get to slip it into the tube.

Teacher: All right. Denise is not ready yet.

Linda: And then you take a measuring cup.

Teacher: Does it matter what size the measuring cup is?

Linda: It doesn't matter.

Teacher: It doesn't matter? Okay.

Denisha: I will take a—

Teacher: So, take a measuring cup and do what?

Denisha: You can use the big one, right? . . . next to clean it.

Linda: *(Inaudible.)*

Teacher: So, yours is stuck, yes?

Linda: It's more easier that way a lot, and then this is sticking up.

Teacher: So, lay the baster in the water, and hold the tube part?

Linda: Yes.

Teacher: Okay. So, I see everybody is doing that.

Linda: And then you fill it up with water.

Teacher: So, you fill it up with water?

Linda: And you get there to dump the water inside *(inaudible)*.

Teacher: So, when you dump the water in and go . . . you're saying that it goes all the way into the tube?

Denisha: See with mine, mine goes that way up.

Teacher: Then watch where the water is going. Oh, wow. Look at that. Look. Look what's in there?

Linda: It's stopped.

Teacher: Look. Look what's happening at the bottom.

Linda: It's making bubbles.

Child: Hey, stop wetting me.

Teacher: Wow!

Denisha: Oh, it's filled up—it's filled up.

Teacher: Which reminds me of something. You know what Ronnie told me? Ronnie told me that if you put the baster under the water, and then you squeeze it, and you squeeze it again, it makes bubbles. So I'm wondering if that's the same thing that's happening with the tube. Is that what's happening? Is that what's happening?

Linda: It seems to.

Teacher: You think so? I wonder if the same thing will happen with the little tube. Why not disconnect *(inaudible)* for a minute? Oh, no. It doesn't fit.

Linda: Same size.

Teacher: Right.

Linda: Same size.

Teacher: It's the same size so it won't fit together. I liked that idea. That was a great idea, because you know what it reminded me of? It reminded me of working together. That Linda had an idea, and Denisha had tried it out, and then we all tried it out, and we saw bubbles.

ADVANCED WORKSHOP 9: VIGNETTE OBSERVATION FORM

Note your observations by identifying the teacher strategies and child responses in separate columns.

Child Behavior/Comments	Teacher Response

READ AND REFLECT 9

Name: _____

Before coming to workshop 9: "Deepening Children's Science Understandings," read about the teacher's role in "Resources" (p. 97) and excerpts from a teacher's journal (p. 10), both in the teacher's guide. Respond to these questions as you reflect on what you read.

1. In what ways did the teacher in the excerpts from a teacher's journal encourage the children's exploration? What strategies did she use? Note exactly what she did and the date of the entry.

2. In what ways did the teacher deepen children's science understanding? What strategies did she use? Note exactly what she did and the date of the entry.

3. In what ways did the teacher promote early math and literacy learning? What strategies did she use? Note exactly what she did and the date of the entry.

Using Books to Extend Science Learning

AT A GLANCE

Purpose:

- Learn how to select books and use them to enrich children's exploration of water
- Learn to use books that stimulate science inquiry and learning

Activity	Time: 1½ hours	Materials
Examine use of books to enrich children's exploration of water Guide teachers as they examine different categories of books and consider the varied ways books can enrich children's investigations.	20 minutes	• Chart: "Strategies for the Use of Books"
Provide overview of how to use books Review the types of books that might be used in an exploration of water, the role of books in science and literacy learning, and ways for using books.	25 minutes	• Overhead projector, screen, and overheads 10.1–10.3
Evaluate books about water Guide teachers as they evaluate selected books for classroom use. Encourage them to focus their evaluation as they plan for the use of one book.	45 minutes	• Sample books • Copies of "Small Group Discussion about Books"

Pre-assignment: Have teachers bring books they have been using that are related to water. Read the sections on extensions and books for children in the teacher's guide (see p. 92).

Advanced Workshop 10:
Using Books to Extend Science Learning

OBJECTIVES

- Learn how to select books and use them to enrich children's exploration of water
- Learn how to use books to stimulate science inquiry and learning

OVERVIEW

- Examine use of books to enrich children's exploration of water (25 minutes)
- Provide overview of how to use books (20 minutes)
- Evaluate books about water (45 minutes)

INSTRUCTOR PREPARATION

- **GIVE ASSIGNMENT TO TEACHERS.** At least a week before the workshop, tell teachers you want them to read the sections on extensions and books for children in the teacher's guide, and to bring a few (three to five) books they have been using in their water exploration.
- **COLLECT BOOKS IN EACH OF THE CATEGORIES.** To ensure having a variety of books available, collect some on your own.

MATERIALS

- Three to four books from each of the following categories (note: see pp. 106–110 of the teacher's guide for a list of recommended books within each category):
    - Nonfiction: informational books, image books, and biographies
    - Fiction: fact and fantasy, real-life fiction
    - Poetry books
- Copies of "Small Group Discussion about Books"
- Chart: "Strategies for the Use of Books" with two columns: "Book Title" and "Strategies for Use"
- Overhead projector, screen, and overheads 10.1–10.3

Activity

EXAMINE USE OF BOOKS TO ENRICH CHILDREN'S EXPLORATION (25 MINUTES)

PURPOSE: This interactive sharing will acknowledge the teachers' current work and encourage collaboration that might be extended outside the workshop setting.

1. **Introduce the workshop** (5 minutes). Begin the workshop by mentioning the importance of books—their value to literacy development as well as science learning. Provide an overview of the content of this workshop. Confirm that the teachers have brought some books with them.

2. **Ask participants to share books they have used as part of the their exploration of water** (20 minutes). Focus the discussion on how teachers chose these books, what they hoped the children would gain, and how they have used them. Allow enough time for teachers to share one of their books. Ask for specifics with questions such as the following:

   - When did you introduce this book in the exploration and why?

   - How did you use this book with children? What did you accomplish?

   - How did the children respond?

   Write titles and their uses on the prepared chart. Look for uses such as the following:

   - Children became interested in the streams on the playground after a rain

   - This book prepared children to take on the challenge of building clay boats

   - Children are experimenting with paint as a way to represent water

> It is possible that teachers might suggest inappropriate books or book uses and you may not want to address these right now. Note them on the chart and return to the chart at the end of the workshop. Compare the list to those uses they learned about. This would be a good time to question ones that may not belong. You might ask, "Does this fit with what we have just learned?" Be prepared with a rationale for taking it off the chart in case it is not obvious to the teachers.

Provide Overview of How to Use Books (20 minutes)

Purpose: Help teachers understand the role books can play in learning, and the different kinds of books that are important for use.

Show overheads to begin. As you show them, provide examples of books that relate to the points you are making.

Overhead 10.1: Science Books and Science Learning

- **Stimulate science inquiry and thinking**
  Books can heighten children's observation of water in the classroom and in their daily lives—the water coming out of a sprinkler or dripping from a faucet, the puddles after a rain, the way it flows through the tubes in the water table.

- **Provide images and examples of careers in science**
  Books provide children with examples of careers in which science knowledge is important, such as an engineer, plumber, or boat builder.

- **Provide information and ideas relevant to children's scientific inquiries**
  If we look closely at these pictures, can we figure out what shape their boat is? Look at the way the water is coming out of that hose. Can we make it come out of our tubes that way?

- **Connect science exploration with the world outside the classroom**
Most books that reflect images or text about water will help children make connections to the outside world, such as with rivers, the rain, or boats.

OVERHEAD 10.2: SCIENCE BOOKS AND LITERACY DEVELOPMENT

- **Build language skills**
Books introduce children to new vocabulary and contribute to conceptual understandings. They stimulate children's use of language as the children question, explain, and retell the stories.

- **Introduce many genres of books about science**
Use of varied genres expands children's understanding of books, the kinds of language used in books, and various uses of books. At this point you might review the kinds of fiction, nonfiction, and poetry books that are talked about in the teacher's guide or show examples. Be sure everyone understands these distinctions.

- **Engage children with print**
Books are one of the many experiences we want children to have that will contribute to their growing understanding of print. At first many children think that the pictures convey the story. An important learning goal for the preschool years is building the understanding that print also conveys a message and print is made up of letters and words.

- **Develop a love of books**
The connection of books to a science topic that is interesting to the children contributes to their love of books and their desire to use books in varied ways.

OVERHEAD 10.3: USES OF BOOKS ABOUT WATER

- **To read aloud and discuss**
Facilitate conversations in which children discuss ideas presented in books, compare ideas or images from several sources (such as books, posters, or their own experiences), and critically analyze the feasibility of ideas presented in books. Books are a great way to help children connect the daily water experiences they have with what they are doing in the classroom.

- **To read aloud as introduction to a new idea or challenge**
Books can be used to introduce a new challenge such as boat building or idea such as boats sinking or tipping over.

- **To look at and talk about**
Many books that you will find to stimulate children's water investigations will not be appropriate for reading aloud. Often this will be because they have great pictures but the text is too long and detailed or just not interesting. But sitting with a child or small group of children and looking at the pictures and talking about them is a great activity. It will lead children to some new insights about their work, stimulate them to look at water more closely, and connect it to their daily encounters with water.

- **To encourage descriptive language and representation**
Books have descriptive ways of talking about water, its properties and movement. Point this language out to children and give them opportunities to create their own descriptions. Illustrations from books can also be used to help children think about ways of representing water.

EVALUATE BOOKS ABOUT WATER (45 MINUTES)

PURPOSE: Help teachers identify ways they can use different kinds of books to enrich children's exploration of water.

1. **PROVIDE INSTRUCTIONS AND TIME FOR THE SMALL GROUP TASK** (20 minutes). Ask participants to form small groups of three or four. Give each group several books, all from the same category (so one group will have information books, another image books, and so on). Also distribute the "Small Group Discussion about Books" handout. Ask groups to look through their books and use the questions on the handout to discuss how they might use this type of book with children. Finally, they should make a plan for one book in particular. Mention that one person in each group should serve as a recorder. Allow twenty minutes for this small group activity.

2. **FACILITATE GROUP REPORTS** (25 minutes). The amount of time depends somewhat on how many groups you have. Try to structure the time so each group has time to give a report.

   Bring the whole group together. Ask one person from each group to share key points that were raised during their small group discussions and a few ideas about how they would use one of the books.

You may want to highlight the following points during the whole group debriefing:

- There are all kinds of books with pictures of water. Among them are books about weather, rivers, plumbers, and playing outdoors. Use these kinds of books to highlight their connections with water, children's observation of water in and out of school, and to think about their explorations in new ways.

- Water and the ways it can be described are easily translated into poetry. Use this rich language to help children build their capacity for communicating their ideas about water. Ask questions such as, "I like the way the stream is described. Can you think of other words that would describe the way it sounds? How it moves?"

- It can be difficult for children to represent water and its movement. Book illustrations can open new possibilities for them. Talk about the pictures, giving the children an opportunity to imagine how they were made and which materials were used. Provide opportunities for children to use the same materials.

- Display books about water in a place that is easily accessible to the children.

Conclude by reviewing the different categories of books that appear on pp. 106–110 of the teacher's guide. Suggest that teachers use the list of recommended books, choosing from each of the categories to enrich their exploration. Inform teachers of when and where the next training activity will be.

Suggested Next Steps

- If you want to further pursue the ways that inquiry-based science promotes literacy development, you might offer the representation workshops.

- Plan guided discussions that provide an opportunity for teachers to deepen children's experiences with books.

- Conduct observations of teachers when they are using books. Have a follow-up conference, helping teachers examine their practice.

- Suggest reading from the references:

  Learning to Read and Write: Developmentally Appropriate Practices for Young Children, by the National Association for the Education of Young Children (NAEYC, 1998).

SMALL GROUP DISCUSSION ABOUT BOOKS

Use these questions to guide your small group discussion.

1. What are the special features of this type of book (such as provides accurate information, photos offer realistic images, illustrations are beautiful, and so on)?

2. When would you use this type of book with children?

3. How might you use this type of book to enrich children's explorations of water?

4. What do you think are some of the benefits of using this type of book with children (namely, what can children gain)?

5. Is this book scientifically accurate? If not, how would you deal with that?

Assessing Children's Science Learning

AT A GLANCE

Purpose:

- Become familiar with the assessment tools in the teacher's guide
- Practice using the observation records and plan for their systematic use

Activity	Time: 1½ hours	Materials
Provide overview of assessment tools in the teacher's guide Offer a framework for assessing children's science learning—its purpose and the process.	15 minutes	• Overhead projector, screen, and overhead 11.1
Practice observing children's water exploration Use the observation record form to assess children's science learning.	45 minutes	• Chart: "Observing Children's Water Exploration" • VCR, monitor, and video cued to vignette 5 • Copies of observation record and transcript to vignette 5 (used in workshop 9)
Relate to teachers' practice Discuss ways teachers can systematically use the observation record and the learning record to regularly assess children's inquiry skills and science understandings.	30 minutes	

Pre-assignment: Read the "Observation and Assessment" section in the teacher's guide (see p. 100). Use the observation record form in the teacher's guide to document what children say and do during a water exploration.

Advanced Workshop 11:
Assessing Children's Science Learning

OBJECTIVES

- Become familiar with the assessment tools in the teacher's guide
- Practice using the observation records and plan for their systematic use

OVERVIEW

- Provide overview of assessment tools in the teacher's guide (15 minutes)
- Practice observing children's exploration of water (45 minutes)
- Relate assessment to teachers' practice (30 minutes)

INSTRUCTOR PREPARATION

- **REVIEW VIGNETTE 5.** View it and note the aspects that you will highlight during the workshop. This vignette is also used in workshop 9.

MATERIALS

- Chart: "Observing Children's Water Exploration"
- VCR, monitor, and video cued to vignette 5
- Overhead projector, screen, and overhead 11.1
- Copies of transcript to vignette 5 (used in workshop 9) and an observation record form for each teacher

Activity

PROVIDE OVERVIEW OF ASSESSMENT IN SCIENCE EXPLORATIONS (15 MINUTES)

PURPOSE: This activity will set the stage for those that follow by providing an assessment framework for science learning, its purpose and process.

1. **INTRODUCE THE WORKSHOP AND DISCUSS THE PURPOSE OF ASSESSMENT** (5 minutes). Give an overview of the activities. Ask teachers why they think assessment is important and what it involves. Allow them to share their ideas, reinforcing those that refer to assessment as a way to make informed decisions about teaching and learning. Emphasize these points:

   - Assessment provides information about children's interests, abilities, and understandings
   - Ultimately, the teacher learns about the effectiveness of her teaching through assessment
   - Assessment is ongoing and the process includes documentation, reflection, and planning

2. Introduce the key elements of the assessment process using overhead 11.1 (5 minutes).

Overhead 11.1: Key Elements of the Assessment Process

- **Collecting data**
  You might want to ask teachers what they think data means in this context. Emphasize the value of regularly collecting multiple sources of data (written observations, photographs, video- and audiotape, or samples of children's work) that can provide insights about children's inquiry skills and their understandings of the science concepts. Suggest that teachers document at least one observation per child every two weeks, and collect one work sample per child per week.

- **Analyzing data regularly**
  This data will only have meaning when teachers take time to think about it. Teachers should examine varied documents to gauge each child's engagement and science learning. At the same time, teachers should look at the class as a whole and where it is going.

- **Drawing conclusions and making decisions**
  Conclusions are about the important links between teaching and learning. Are your children engaged? Are they deepening their understanding of the science concepts by using inquiry? Are all children making progress? What does this mean for your teaching? These are the key questions that will lead to conclusions and making informed decisions about next steps.

---

3. Ask teachers to open their teacher's guides to "Science Outcomes: Science Inquiry Skills and Science Concepts" (5 minutes) in the appendices (pp. 120–121). Review the chart with them, pointing out the kinds of information it provides. Explain that they will use this chart as a basis for assessing children's science learning.

Practice Observing Children's Water Explorations (45 minutes)

Purpose: This activity will help teachers learn what to look for as they observe and document their observations using the observation record form. Such an activity will help teachers focus on science concepts and inquiry skills as they assess children's learning.

1. Observe and discuss vignette 5 (45 minutes).

  a. Start by asking the teachers what they look for as they assess their children's engagement and understandings. Note their ideas on the chart, "Observing Children's Water Exploration." Add important ideas that they do not mention.

> Look for ideas such as whether or not the children are showing interest and staying with an activity, the aspects of inquiry they are using, the ways they are communicating ideas, the ideas they have, and the quality of their interaction with other children.

  b. Introduce vignette 5 by saying that it was filmed at a Boston class for four- and five-year-olds. Tell them that they will be watching the vignette twice; the second time they will take notes.

c. Show the vignette. Then ask teachers what they noticed about the children's engagement and their understandings. Listen to their comments, asking for specifics and keeping teachers focused on what they actually saw—not their interpretation of it. Highlight any differences of opinion or questions.

d. Prepare for the next viewing by passing out the observation record form and transcript. Remind them that their notes should be objective—not interpretations. Also encourage them to use the outcomes chart to focus their observations.

e. Show the vignette again. Then ask teachers what they noticed this time. During the conversation, highlight important aspects of documenting observations:

- Document—Complete and objective notes are critical. Have some teachers tell the class what they wrote. You might want to take one small sequence and get a couple of variations, working toward a more complete statement. (Mention that this is similar to one major goal for children—to observe and describe what they see.)

- Analyze—Consider the variations in children's engagement and understandings that come when you begin to interpret the observation notes. Reflecting on what children say and do provides insights into their level of engagement and their science understandings. In this vignette, all four children are actively engaged in using basters and tubes to explore water and its flow: they seem to be in the early stages of using these materials. Ronnie is just learning how to fill the baster and use the bulb to get water to come out. Both Ronnie and Linda discover ways of producing bubbles. They are not yet ready to predict when bubbles will occur or generalize across bubble experiences. While Linda can articulately describe her process step by step, Ronnie is not as able to talk about what he is doing. Denisha shows ability to collaborate as she acknowledges Linda's discovery and works to re-create it herself.

- Plan—Observations can help teachers plan next steps. For example, seeing these two ways of producing bubbles can help a teacher prepare for some recording of data, preparing further investigation, and new discussions about bubble making.

Relate Assessment to Teachers' Practice (30 minutes)

Purpose: This is an opportunity for the teachers to connect their new understandings about assessment to their own classroom practice. They can also look for ways to incorporate the assessment tools into their ongoing work.

1. Conduct an informal conversation (20 minutes). Ask teachers how they have connected this approach to their own assessment practices. Use the following questions to focus their comments (continue to reference the outcomes chart):

- What kind of science engagement do you see in your classrooms? Let teachers talk about what they are seeing for a few minutes. Then ask them to examine the science concepts (noted on the outcomes chart) being explored and the inquiry their children are engaged in.

- In what ways have you recorded your observations? For instance, teachers may place clipboards around the room with copies of the observation record form so they are always available. Also, encourage use of multimedia, including audio and video recording, because such methods capture moments that allow for deeper reflection. Elicit issues teachers have with the process and encourage them to help each other resolve barriers they encounter. For example, talk about how they might use the observation record form regularly.

- Are you systematically analyzing your data? Find out when they are finding time for reflection, letting them learn from each other. Allow issues to surface and help teachers find solutions. Be sure they understand that observations and other documents become more valuable if they are used for assessment purposes, informing teaching on a regular basis.

2. **INTRODUCE THE OBSERVATION RECORD FORM** (10 minutes) by asking them to turn to p. 116 in their teacher's guides. Explain that this is a way of recording science inquiry and understandings over the period of one exploration. Mention that the outcomes will help them with the meaning of some of these items. Use Ronnie as an example and ask what might be noted about him based on this one observation. While you cannot distinguish "sometimes" and "consistently," you can identify things that he reveals about his understandings and inquiry skills. Look for ideas such as beginning to recognize the impact of force on water, or provides one-sentence responses to questions about his work and uses descriptive vocabulary with words such as bubbles, under water, or spray.

3. **CONCLUDE** by sharing the topic of the next workshop and when it is scheduled. Give teachers any assignment you want them to complete in preparation.

Suggested Next Steps

- Follow up with individual teachers to see if they are finding ways to use the assessment tools in their classrooms. Key to their success with the tools is their ability to make sense of the science in their children's explorations. Look for any issues they might have with the science and provide support when needed. One strategy is to observe with them and talk about the science being explored. Another would be to view vignettes and just talk about the science understandings evident in each one.

- The representation and documentation panel workshops all reinforce ideas about assessment.

- Use upcoming guided discussions to examine and discuss what children's work samples and conversations reveal about their level of engagement, inquiry skills, and science understandings.

- Suggest readings from the references:

"The Role of the Constructivist Teacher," chapter 4 in *The Young Child as Scientist: A Constructivist Approach to Early Childhood Science Education*, by C. Chaille and L. Britain (Allyn & Bacon, 2003).

Learning in Science: The Implications of Children's Science, by R. Osborne and P. Freyberg (Heinemann, 1985).

Encouraging Representation

AT A GLANCE

Purpose:

- Gain an understanding of the purpose of observational drawing and other forms of representation in young children's science learning
- Identify strategies for encouraging representation
- Practice assessing children's representations
- Learn to select and display appropriate representation materials

Activity	Time: 1½ hours	Materials
Provide overview of the role of representation in inquiry science Use overheads to introduce this session and discuss how representation can promote children's science learning.	15 minutes	• Overhead projector, screen, and overheads 12.1 and 12.2
Discuss encouraging representation through conversation Use a video vignette to discuss the ways a teacher can support representation.	30 minutes	• VCR, monitor, and video cued to vignette 6 • Chart: "Strategies for Encouraging Representation" • Copies of workshop 12 vignette observation form and transcript to vignette 6
Discuss encouraging representation—environment and routines Facilitate a conversation about appropriate representation materials and how to make them accessible to the children during their exploration. Share the importance of regular routines.	15 minutes	
Help teachers assess children's representations Guide teachers as they analyze overheads of children's work, using the document annotation form from the teacher's guide.	30 minutes	• Overheads 12.3–12.8 • Copies of document annotation form

Post-assignment: Review the section on representation in "The Teacher's Role," which appears on p. 97 of the teacher's guide.

Advanced Workshop 12: Encouraging Representation

OBJECTIVES

- Gain an understanding of the purpose of observational drawing and other forms of representation in young children's science learning
- Identify strategies for encouraging representation
- Practice assessing children's representations
- Learn to select and display appropriate materials

OVERVIEW

- Provide overview of the role of representation (15 minutes)
- Discuss encouraging representation through conversations (30 minutes)
- Discuss encouraging representation—environment and routines (15 minutes)
- Help teachers assess children's representations (30 minutes)

INSTRUCTOR PREPARATION

- **GIVE ASSIGNMENT.** At least one week before the workshop ask teachers to review the section on representation that appears in "Resources" on p. 111 of the teacher's guide.
- **REVIEW VIGNETTE 6.** View the vignette and note teaching strategies that you will highlight in the workshop.

MATERIALS

- Copies of document annotation form
- Overhead projector, screen, and overheads 12.1–12.8
- VCR, monitor, and video cued to vignette 6
- Chart: "Strategies for Encouraging Representation"
- Copies of workshop 12 vignette observation form and transcript to vignette 6

Activity

PROVIDE OVERVIEW OF THE ROLE OF REPRESENTATION (15 MINUTES)

PURPOSE: Understanding how representation can promote children's inquiry and science understandings will be key to the teacher's work with children. This overview will also set the stage for the rest of this workshop.

1. **INTRODUCE THE WORKSHOP AND PROVIDE AN OVERVIEW** of the purpose of representation in science teaching and learning (5 minutes). Provide an overview of the activities in this workshop. Show overhead 12.1. Note that Makayla has drawn the circles she saw as drops landed. Use the following discussion points to talk about the purpose of representation:

- Encourages children to look closely at water: the ways it moves through tubes or falls as rain, how it looks in containers, or as drops on paper.

- Builds abilities to use multiple media to communicate observations and ideas.

- Encourages new questions.

- Promotes early literacy.

- Supports reflection and theory development.

2. **TALK ABOUT YOUNG CHILDREN AND REPRESENTATION FOR A FEW MINUTES** (10 minutes). Show overhead 12.2 (Alex's perspective on rain falling) and make the following points:

- Three- and four-year-olds are just learning to draw. Their motor abilities are not fully developed and they are just learning about symbolic representation.

- Children's early representations often focus on just one characteristic. When drawing drops they might be interested in size, shape, or quantity but are unable to think about multiple characteristics at the same time. Referring to overhead 12.2, mention that Alex has represented rain as many drops while Makayla has given them more size and shape. Make the point that it is a mistake to do too much interpreting without getting the child's thoughts about what they have done.

- Children need available tools and plenty of time to practice. Clipboards that are easily accessible are useful for making representations.

- Each child will have their own preference for the medium in which they choose to communicate. In part, this is developmental—can they grasp a big marker or pen? It may also be a difference in style. Some children prefer three-dimensional representation, such as clay or collage, and others prefer movement.

- It is important to select media that allow children to represent the science they are exploring. Water movement is particularly difficult. Movement and demonstration are often the best methods at the beginning. Paint is another good medium. You might provide collage cutouts of funnels and tubes and yarn or tissue paper for the water. Children can also learn to use things such as arrows to show the direction of the water flow.

DISCUSS ENCOURAGING REPRESENTATION THROUGH CONVERSATIONS (30 MINUTES)

PURPOSE: Teachers will generate a list of strategies they can use to encourage representation in their own classrooms.

1. **DISCUSS THE READING ASSIGNMENT** (10 minutes). Ask, "What are some important points about encouraging representation mentioned in the teacher's guide?" List these ideas on the chart you prepared. Encourage teachers to think about how different parts of the guide (such as the teacher's role, open exploration, and focused exploration) support their work with children around representation.

2. **INTRODUCE AND SHOW VIGNETTE 6** (20 minutes). Start by saying that this vignette shows a teacher and a small group of children exploring drops. They will see the teacher introducing the exploration, the children making drops on different surfaces, representing drops with two media (clay and drawing), and sharing their work. Distribute the workshop 12

vignette observation form and the transcript, and ask teachers to note strategies the teacher in the video uses to encourage representation and engage children with science. Mention that the vignette shows more than the representation. They should watch for what the teacher might be doing at any point in time that contributes to the representation process for the children.

Show the vignette and ask teachers what they noticed. Note their strategies on the chart you prepared. Ask how these strategies promote science learning, what their connection is to inquiry, and the science concepts.

Look for ideas like these:

- Encourages children to focus on specific features of the drops throughout the process. This begins with the introduction when she asks them to predict what the drops will look like—their movement and shape. She continues this focus during the exploration and representation process, in particular with the child working with clay. Attention to size and shape before representing helps children attend to these details while they are representing. In addition, the process of re-creating drops with pen or clay heightens their focus on these details.

- Asks children to represent, provides materials, and gives simple instructions.

- Shows value for their work through her presence and encouragement.

Discuss Encouraging Representation— Environment and Routines (15 minutes)

Purpose: An important part of encouraging representation is the choice of materials and their accessibility, as well as regular routines. This conversation will highlight key strategies.

1. **Talk about the selection of materials for a few minutes** (5 minutes). Ask teachers how the selection of materials can encourage representation. Note their strategies on the chart, seeing that the following points are made:

   - Materials must be selected that allow for representation of the important characteristics of the object or motion being represented. For example, drawing is a medium that allows for representation of characteristics such as size and shape but only two dimensions. The amount of detail possible varies with the type of pen or marker being used. Fine-tip markers allow for more detail. Remind teachers that they will need to help children find ways to represent the direction and movement of the water. Mention that their expectations should be in line with the medium's potential.

   - Varied materials should be available. Consider both two- and three-dimensional material as important. A collage can be useful for showing the setup of the materials and the flow of the water. Clay is an effective way of representing drops, allowing for consideration of size and shape. Drawing is also valuable, but children might focus on the materials the water is in rather than the water itself. Teachers will need to encourage the next step—what the water looks like in these materials. Some teachers begin by representing the materials themselves and having the children add the water. This allows the children to focus on the challenge of representing movement and the way the water appears in the container.

- Books can be used as a stimulus by talking about ways that illustrators have represented water. Illustrations might suggest other medium to try, such as watercolors.

- Charts are another way to use representation to collect data. For example, the teacher might draw a tub of water and have the children draw the placement of objects they put in the water during a sink and float activity. A document like this can be used later during an analysis conversation—"Why do you think these objects all sank? Are they alike in any way?"

- Movement and demonstration can be effective means of representation. Allow children to use their arms and hands to show the way in which the water flowed, or to use the baster, tubes, and funnels to show what they did.

2. **TALK ABOUT THE IMPORTANCE OF ACCESSIBILITY** (2 to 3 minutes). Ask teachers how to display materials so they can inspire representation. Be sure to make the following points:

- Children should be able to get materials and put them back without help.

- Materials should be available in or next to the places where they are exploring water so it can be directly connected with their observations.

- Clipboards are especially useful for drawing in places where a hard surface is not available. They may also help keep paper dry if the water is close at hand.

- Representation should be done when the water and materials being represented are in view.

3. **TALK ABOUT THE IMPORTANCE OF REGULAR ROUTINES** (5 minutes). Ask teachers how regular routines support children's representation. Note their strategies on the chart and be sure to make the following points:

- Regular encouragement from the teacher, with reminders or suggestions, can help children make representation a part of their routine. Give a few examples such as, "Would you like to draw a picture of the way you put the hose through the wire wall to help you remember it?" or "I have some clay. Would you like to use it to make these drops?"

- Large group time is a good time to show that you value children's work by sharing it.

4. **FINALLY, TALK ABOUT DISPLAYING CHILDREN'S WORK** (2 to 3 minutes). Make these points about things teachers should consider as they display children's work:

- Displaying children's work shows that you value what they do.

- Displays allow children to revisit their work and build on their ideas.

- Displays should be at the children's eye level.

- Displays should reflect children's current interests and investigations.

- Displays can be a powerful way to educate parents about the important learning that is going on in the classroom.

HELP TEACHERS ASSESS CHILDREN'S REPRESENTATIONS (30 MINUTES)

PURPOSE: This activity will help teachers understand how children represent water. By carefully reflecting on and assessing children's representations, teachers can learn bout children's inquiry skills and their science understanding.

1. **Introduce the activity** (5 minutes). Tell teachers that they will be looking at some children's work samples and talking about the science understandings being communicated. Ask the teachers to open the teacher's guide to the outcomes chart in the appendices. Explain that they will refer to this chart as they assess children's work. Distribute the document annotation forms and refer to their placement in the teacher's guide. Make the following points:

   - Note that using the forms will help teachers focus their analysis of each piece of work. These completed forms can also help families appreciate what their children are learning.

   - Representations are best understood in conjunction with a conversation where the children share their ideas about their work.

2. **Show and discuss overheads** (25 minutes). Show as many overheads (12.3–12.7) as time allows. Ask teachers to talk about what they see and what they might write on a document annotation form.

Overhead 12.3: Tzeidel's Water Flow

Context: Documenting what he has learned about the flow of water in a hose when the hose has been held in three different positions. In this kindergarten class the teacher has drawn the containers for the children and they have represented the water.

Science being explored/evidence: How water moves or flows and how its flow can be changed. Note that he seems to be exploring how the height of both ends of the funnel affects the flow of the water. He may be realizing that the direction of the water flow is from the higher end to the lower one. There also seems to be some understanding that blowing, squirting, or pumping would have different results. Tzeidel is also learning how to record the data from his investigations.

A good discussion topic for the teacher and Tzeidel would be explaining his arrows and exactly what was happening. Did the water spill out? After elaborating the data with his descriptors he could be asked if he noticed any similarities about the behavior of the water in these three situations. He could be asked to draw another setup before doing it and predict how the water would flow. The teacher could ask for thoughts about what the tubes look like when the water stops moving.

Overhead 12.4: Katherine's Water Flow

Context: This sample was collected one month later in the same kindergarten class. The children are now representing the containers as well as the water. The teacher has labeled Katherine's drawing with her.

Science being explored/evidence: Katherine shows water in the shape of its containers and its flow from one container to another. She has not given us any indicators of the direction of the flow of the water, but might be able to explain this if asked. She seems to be investigating the flow of water from one container to another.

The teacher might talk with Katherine about this setup—her rationale for the placement of the blocks and what she learned from doing this. She might wonder if it mattered how much water she used. Do the containers hold the same amount of water? She might ask if Katherine would want to set it up differently next time and why or if there would be a variation in the setup that would make the water flow faster or slower. If she has begun to explore moving water up, she could be given the challenge of seeing if there was a way to get the water to flow from the lower container to the higher one.

OVERHEAD 12.5: BETUL'S DROPS

Context: The children in this childcare center are exploring drops, their shapes, and how they move and stick together on plastic plates.

Science being explored/evidence: Betul is exploring a property of water—it sticks to itself (adhesion). He examines individual drops on the plastic surface and he watches drops move and stick to other drops.

A conversation with Betul might focus on a closer look at the round shape of the drops he has made. They also might talk about whether big drops and little ones look the same.

OVERHEAD 12.6: LUCY'S SPINNING DROPS

Context: This is also a representation of drops.

Science being explored/evidence: Lucy has shown what happens to her drops when she spins her plate—the way the drops stick together and the shape they take when the plate is moved.

A conversation with Lucy might be similar to the one with Betul—comparing her representation with the original, focusing closely on shape and size.

OVERHEAD 12.7: MORE WATER FLOW

Context: This child was using funnels and tubing to explore the properties of water.

This representation is an example of the importance of conversation in encouraging the child's thinking about what they have represented and learned. While it is not obvious from the drawing, this child has carefully shown the funnel, the water flowing out of the tube, and spilling out of the bowl. A conversation might draw out what the child learned from the spilling water.

Show overhead 12.8. Encourage teachers to use this form to annotate photos, work samples, transcripts, or any other documents that they may have. When filling out the form, teachers should highlight what the document reveals about children's exploration of water and their understanding of science concepts. Teachers should attach their annotation to each document. Close by letting the teachers know about the next workshop, as well as the time and location.

Suggested Next Steps

- Make a handout of the strategies and distribute it.
- Follow up with workshop 13, which builds on the content of this workshop.
- Plan guided discussions in which the teachers can share and discuss representations and useful strategies for encouraging representation.
- Conduct observations, helping teachers develop a repertoire of strategies for encouraging representation in their classrooms.
- Suggest readings from the references:

"A Child Constructs an Understanding of a Water Wheel in Five Media," by George Forman (*Childhood Education*, 1996).

"Negotiating with Art Media to Deepen Learning," by George Forman (*Child Care Information Exchange*, 1996).

Observation Drawing with Children: A Framework for Teachers, by N. R. Smith (Teachers College Press, 1998).

TRANSCRIPT OF VIDEO VIGNETTE 6:
FOCUSED EXPLORATION OF DROPS

Scene: This vignette show a small group of children and their teacher engaged in an investigation of drops on different kinds of surfaces. In scenes 1 and 2 the teacher introduces the exploration, encourages predictions, and interacts with the children as they try drops on the surfaces. In scene 3 the teacher gives instructions for representing the drops and two of the children are shown drawing. In scene 4 one child is making clay drops and in scene 5 one of the children is talking about his drawing.

The children: Michael, Nick, Becky, Megan, and Serenity

SCENE 1

Teacher: Today we're going to use the eyedroppers in water with different material. And I'm going to give everyone one piece of material and I'd like you to think about when you drop the water with the eyedropper what shape it's going to make, the little drop of water in the movement. If you think you're going to be able to move the drop of water on the material. So Michael you think about this one.

Teacher: Michael, do you have any ideas?

Michael: Stick.

Teacher: You think it's going to stick. You think it's going to stick? Okay. What about the movement? How do you think it's going to move? You think you'll be able to move it or do you think it's just going to go flat?

Michael: Flat.

Teacher: You think it'll be flat. So you probably wouldn't be able to move it around like Nick did on the paper plate.

Michael: *(Shrugs.)*

Teacher: It's just a guess—we're just going to take a guess and try it out.

Michael: Guess so.

Teacher: You think it might move. Okay. Nick?

Nick: Dissolve.

Teacher: What's it going to do?

Nick: Dissolve.

Teacher: It's going to dissolve. Okay. Is it going to have any shape you think?

Nick: *(Nods no.)*

Teacher: No shape at all. What about the movement?

Nick: *(Nods no.)* Probably it's just going to go right into the Styrofoam.

Teacher: Right into there. Becky?

Becky: It's going to be flat.

Teacher: Flat. So what about the movement? You think there will be any movement and once you put it down and try to move the drop.

Becky: Move.

Teacher: You think it will move—okay.

Becky: *(Nods yes.)*

SCENE 2

Megan: Bigger!

Teacher: That's a bigger one.

Megan: See . . .

Teacher: What's it look like when you use your magnifying glass? What shape is that?

Michael: Mine's kinda round.

Teacher: Kinda round.

Megan: Look.

Teacher: What shape is this, Megan?

Megan: Circle.

Teacher: How about you, Becky? What shape?

Becky: Round.

Teacher: Round. Did you try picking it up and moving it? Oh, I see what Becky's doing. Can you tell us what you're doing, Becky?

Becky: I'm dragging the bubbles over to the other bubbles.

Teacher: And what's happening?

Becky: It's making a big bubble.

Teacher: It is.

Teacher: How are you doing, Nick?

Nick: Good.

Teacher: Did the drops go into that material like you thought they would?

Nick: Uh-huh.

Teacher: Is it going through or is it just wet on the top?

Nick: It's going through. *(Turns it over to look at other side.)*

SCENE 3

Teacher: If you could just maybe draw a picture of something you just did with the material you had and the drops . . . maybe the shape of the drops . . . how the drops landed . . . the movement . . . any ideas.

(Michael and Megan are shown drawing.)

SCENE 4

Teacher: Do you think that you could make me some of those on here? Do this and make the shape of the drop like this.

Serenity: How about a tiny one?

Teacher: If you look at the shape of this.

Serenity: Here, that one *(showing teacher small drop of clay).*

Teacher: Maybe you can make me a small one and a big one.

(Serenity makes and shows tiny drop of clay to teacher.)

Teacher: That is a tiny one. Let's set it over there. Are you finished with it? You don't want to lose it. So these are the shape of these? *(Points to clay and then drops.)* Okay. Maybe you can do a few more here? That must be a bigger one. That does kind of look like that shape right there. *(Points to the clay and drops again.)* It's good.

SCENE 5

Teacher: Okay, Michael.

Michael: That's the eyedropper, that's the tape, this is the table, and these little things are the bubbles. This is the, um . . .

Michael: These are the other bubbles. This is my bowl of water.

Teacher: Your bowl of water. Can you tell us something about your drops?

Michael: Trying to make them round.

Teacher: What is this? Can you tell me about this? That's interesting.

Michael: Eyedropper . . . *(inaudible)*

Teacher: Is there anything else you'd like to share, Michael? Would you like to tell us anything about the drops? The movement or the shape?

Michael: Round.

Teacher: They were round. Did they move?

Michael: Some of them moved. The big ones moved, the little ones didn't.

Teacher: And I noticed you were trying to make little, little tiny drops. How did you make that little tiny drop?

Michael: Squeezed it gently.

Teacher: You squeezed it gently. So, if you squeezed it gently you got a little drop. And what if you squeezed it harder? What would happen?

Child: A little drop.

Teacher: So you think so—a little drop if you squeezed it harder? What do you think, Michael? If you squeezed the eyedropper harder, would you get a little drop or a larger drop?

Michael: Big.

Teacher: A big one. Is there anything else you'd like to share?

Michael: Guess that's it.

Teacher: Thank you, Michael.

ADVANCED WORKSHOP 12: VIGNETTE OBSERVATION FORM

Note your observations by identifying the teacher strategies and child responses in separate columns.

Child Behavior/Comments	Teacher Response

Using Children's Representations as Teaching Tools

AT A GLANCE

Purpose:
- Examine the ways representation can be used to deepen children's science learning
- Have science talks about children's representations

Activity	Time: 1½ hours	Materials
Help teachers assess children's representations Working in small groups, help teachers assess representations from their own classrooms.	30 minutes	• Copies of document annotations
Discuss using representations as teaching tools Use vignettes to help teachers identify strategies for using representations to deepen children's science understandings.	35 minutes	• Chart: "Strategies for Talking about Representations" • VCR, monitor, and video cued to vignette 6 • Overhead projector, screen, and overheads 12.8 and 13.1 • Copies of workshop 13 vignette observation form and transcripts to vignette 6 (used in workshop 12)
Help teachers use children's representations to stimulate science talks Support teachers as they plan goals and questions for a conversation with one of their children about their representation.	25 minutes	• Copies of "Representation Conversation Planning Form"

Pre-assignment: Bring at least three observational drawings or other forms of representation (such as collage) to the workshop.

Advanced Workshop 13:
Using Children's Representations as Teaching Tools

OBJECTIVES

- Examine the ways representation can be used to deepen children's science learning
- Plan science talks about children's representations

OVERVIEW

- Help teachers assess children's representations (30 minutes)
- Discuss using representations as teaching tools (35 minutes)
- Help teachers use representation to plan a science talk (25 minutes)

INSTRUCTOR PREPARATION

- **GIVE ASSIGNMENT.** At least one week before the workshop, ask teachers to collect three to five representations from their class. Suggest diversity, either in children's ability or in the medium used.
- **REVIEW VIGNETTE 6.** View the vignette, noting aspects you will highlight in the workshop.

> The activities in this workshop assume that teachers have already participated in advanced workshop 12. In workshop 12, they learn to fill out document annotations, and in this workshop they start using them to assess their own children's work.

MATERIALS

- Chart: "Strategies for Talking about Representation"
- VCR, monitor, and video cued to vignette 6
- Overhead projector, screen, and overheads 12.8 and 13.1
- Copies of document annotation form (two for each teacher), transcript to vignette 6, science talk planning form, workshop 13 vignette observation form, and representation conversation planning form

Activity

HELP TEACHERS ASSESS CHILDREN'S REPRESENTATIONS (30 MINUTES)

PURPOSE: This activity will help teachers apply what they are learning as they assess what children's representations reveal about their science understandings.

1. **INTRODUCE THE WORKSHOP AND FIRST TASK** (5 minutes). Provide an overview of the workshop activities. Then show overhead 12.8—the sample document annotation form—and review how to fill one out. Pass out two forms to everyone and ask them to select two of

the samples they brought that show distinctly different medium or skill levels. Suggest they refer to the outcomes chart in the resources section of the teacher's guide to complete a document annotation form for each of the two samples they have selected. Ask them to form questions on another piece of paper. Tell teachers they have twenty minutes to complete this task.

2. **SUPPORT TEACHERS AS THEY COMPLETE THE DOCUMENT ANNOTATION FORMS** (20 minutes). Go around the room and check on individuals. Help them think through what they want to write when they seem stuck. As they complete their forms, ask them to partner with another teacher who is done. Their partners might have additional thoughts as they examine children's representations.

3. **ASK TEACHERS TO SHARE THEIR THOUGHTS ABOUT THIS EXPERIENCE** (5 minutes). Listen to comments and provide support as teachers think through issues. Teachers might say it was easier to assess representation if they had discussions with children about their work. Emphasize how these conversations with children can provide added insights into their work, what they are trying to accomplish, and their science understandings.

USING REPRESENTATIONS AS TEACHING TOOLS (30 MINUTES)

PURPOSE: Talking to children about their representations can help teachers assess children's understandings. Such conversations also provide a teaching opportunity, helping children to reflect on their experiences and their ideas. This activity will help teachers develop a list of strategies for their use.

1. **DISCUSS THE VARIED WAYS REPRESENTATIONS CAN SERVE AS TEACHING TOOLS** (15 minutes). Show overhead 13.1. Point out the term *documentation*, which includes photographs, data charts, dictations, and children's representations.

OVERHEAD 13.1: USE REPRESENTATIONS TO DEEPEN LEARNING AND PROMOTE INQUIRY

- **Build ability to communicate observations and ideas**
  As children talk about their work, encourage them to describe what they have represented. Model using descriptive language yourself.

- **Focus on particular science ideas**
  For example, talk about the path of the water's flow and how it has been represented. You might have the materials used (such as tubes, funnel, or bucket) to look at along with the child's representation.

- **Build a culture of inquiry and collaboration**
  Look at children's work with groups of children. Compare and contrast different strategies for accomplishing the same goal (such as moving water from one bucket to another, making a boat that floats) by highlighting the different ways they have been represented. Highlight a range of methods, such as drawing, movement, and demonstration.

- **Connect children's explorations from one day to the next**
  Use their work to call attention to what they were doing a day or two ago. This will help them continue an investigation, moving forward with their inquiry.

- **Recap what has been learned at key points in an exploration**
  Use selections of several children's work to review what they have done and learned before moving on.

- **Stimulate discussion in which children synthesize and analyze their work**
  Use documents to compare, contrast, and draw conclusions about the properties of water they have been exploring and questions they have.

Transition to the next activity by saying that they will get a chance to apply these ideas as they look at a video vignette.

2. **VIEW AND DISCUSS VIGNETTE 6** (20 minutes). Tell teachers that this is the same vignette they viewed in workshop 12. Distribute the workshop 13 vignette observation form. Tell teachers that as they view the vignette, they should note the strategies being used next to the appropriate box.

   Show the vignette. After viewing, ask teachers to identify strategies (and list on prepared chart) the teacher is using and then talk about other ways these drawings might be used. Every representation does not have a use for each learning goal, so you don't need to fill in every box.

> During the discussion, emphasize how teachers can use representations to deepen children's science understanding and promote inquiry. Look for ideas like these:
>
> - The teacher has made this representation work as an integral part of the investigation. It follows and builds on the exploration itself.
> - Focuses children on characteristics of the drops, including size, shape, and behavior on different surfaces (adhesion and cohesion).
> - It serves as a form of data recording, providing documentation for future reference and sharing of this experience.
> - It is used to stimulate reflection of the experience, what children noticed about the drops and how they were made, and sharing of their particular experiences.
>
> Some other suggestions include the following:
>
> - Together, these representations with dictations from the children could be used to make a documentation panel about drops on different surfaces. When reviewed as a group, the children could use this data to consider what they found and form some ideas about what happens when water is dropped on varied surfaces. They could discuss the characteristics of surfaces that water sinks into, surfaces on which water just spreads out, and characteristics of surfaces on which water forms round or flat drops.
> - They could be used to introduce further exploration of drops. On another day these representations could stimulate other children to engage in this investigation, or they could lead these same children to ask some new questions about water on other surfaces.
> - They might look at drops in books and examine how they have been represented. This might suggest new materials to try (such as watercolors), or call their attention to characteristics that they have not previously noticed.
> - They might lead to a discussion of raindrops—how they appear on different surfaces (such as windows, dirt, flowers, leaves, or their clothes). A walk outside after a rainfall would provide an opportunity for the children to gather some data using representation or describe in words that the teacher writes down. A whole investigation of what kind of protective clothing to wear when it rains could follow. Give the teachers a chance to discuss how this might be investigated using inquiry.

PLANNING A CONVERSATION ABOUT CHILDREN'S REPRESENTATIONS (20 MINUTES)

PURPOSE: This activity will help the teachers apply to their own classroom what they are learning about using representations as teaching tools.

1. **SET UP THIS PLANNING TASK** (5 minutes) by distributing the representation conversation planning form. Tell teachers that you are going to give them a chance to use one of their representations to guide a conversation that furthers children's science learning and promotes inquiry. Review the form and answer any questions they have.

2. **GIVE THEM TEN MINUTES TO WORK.** Wander around the room and help those who seem to be struggling. Focus them on the appropriate science and ways they might help children add details to their discussion of what they saw, comparison of the actual water and what has been represented, or to discuss similarities and differences in how they have represented water in several pieces of work. Encourage teachers to talk to each other as they work.

3. **BRING THEM TOGETHER TO SHARE IDEAS** (5 minutes). Allow a few minutes for a few of them to share ideas and solve any issues that arise. Encourage them to follow through and have this conversation. Make a point of telling teachers that while this workshop is focused on using children's representations, all forms of documentation can be used as teaching tools in this same way. This would include photographs and records of data.

In conclusion, let them know about the next workshop, when and where it takes place, and which assignments they should complete.

Suggested Next Steps

- Make a handout of the strategies list and distribute it.

- You might follow up with a workshop about making documentation panels.

- Conduct guided discussions in which teachers bring documentation (video- or audiotape) of conversations about children's representations, and analyze them together.

- Observe and conference with teachers around a representation conversation.

- Suggest readings from the references:

"Negotiating with Art Media to Deepen Learning," by George Forman (*Child Care Information Exchange*, 1996).

Helping Children Ask Good Questions, by George Forman (Exchange Press, 1996).

ADVANCED WORKSHOP 13: VIGNETTE OBSERVATION FORM

Goal of Strategy	Strategies in Vignette 6
Build capacity to communicate observations and ideas	
Focus on particular science ideas	
Build a culture of inquiry and collaboration	
Connect children's explorations from one day to the next	
Recap what has been learned	
Help children synthesize and analyze their work	

Advanced Workshop 13:
Representation Conversation Planning Form

Name: _____

Child: _____

Goal(s) of conversation: _____

_____

_____

Science content to explore : _____

List a few questions that you can use to get the conversation going, and search for deeper meanings along the way. Note the part of the representation that each question might be focused on—for example, you might want to talk about how the child has shown that the water is moving.

Facilitating Science Talks

AT A GLANCE

Purpose:
- Build an understanding of group conversations and the role they play in children's science learning
- Build various strategies for facilitating science talks
- Build an awareness of what inhibits conversations

Activity	Time: 1½ hours	Materials
Provide an overview of science talks Let teachers share their early attempts at science talks, the successes and issues. Begin to talk about effective and ineffective strategies.	30 minutes	• Charts: "Strategies for Science Talks" and "Issues We Are Having with Science Talks" • Overhead projector, screen, and overheads 14.1–14.3
Help teachers analyze a small group science talk Use a vignette to highlight the importance of science talks and identify strategies teachers can use to facilitate them.	25 minutes	• VCR, monitor, and video cued to vignette 4 • Copies of workshop 14 vignette observation form and transcript to vignette 4 (used in workshop 7)
Help teachers analyze a large group science talk Use a transcript to highlight the importance of large group science talks and identify strategies teachers can use to facilitate them.	35 minutes	• VCR, monitor, and video cued to vignette 7 • Copies of transcript for vignette 7 and "Strategies for Facilitating Science Talks"

Pre-assignment: Participants will be asked to pay attention as they talk with children, noting where they are engaging them in thinking about science and where they are having difficulty. They should also complete "Read and Reflect 14."

Advanced Workshop 14: Facilitating Science Talks

OBJECTIVES

- Build an understanding of group conversations and the role they play in children's science learning
- Build various strategies for facilitating science talks
- Build an awareness of what inhibits conversations

OVERVIEW

- Provide overview of science talks (30 minutes)
- Help teachers analyze a small group science talk (25 minutes)
- Help teachers analyze a large group science talk (35 minutes)

INSTRUCTOR PREPARATION

- **GIVE ASSIGNMENT.** At least one week before the workshop, distribute the "Read and Reflect" assignment. Also ask teachers to pay attention as they talk with children, noting when they are succeeding and where they have difficulty.
- **REVIEW VIGNETTES 4 AND 7.** View the vignettes, noting the aspects you will highlight during the workshop.

MATERIALS

- VCR, monitor, and video cued to vignette 4
- Copies of handouts: vignette observation form, transcripts for vignettes 4 (see workshop 7), "Read and Reflect 14," and "Strategies for Facilitating Science Talks"
- Charts: "Strategies for Science Talks" and "Issues We Are Having with Science Talks"
- Overhead projector, screen, and overheads 14.1–14.3

Activity

PROVIDE OVERVIEW OF SCIENCE TALKS (30 MINUTES)

PURPOSE: This activity will set the stage for analyzing science conversations with young children. It will allow teachers to share their successes and issues, expand their repertoire of strategies, and begin to overcome barriers they may be experiencing.

1. **INTRODUCE THE WORKSHOP** and begin to identify strategies for promoting conversations with children who are exploring water (15 minutes).

   a. Remind teachers of the importance of conversations in building children's understandings. Review these points:

- Conversation stimulates and makes explicit the thinking processes that underlie several aspects of inquiry (such as collecting data, synthesizing and analyzing data, drawing conclusions, making theories, and using language to communicate). It is also an essential aspect of collaboration.

- Sharing ideas stimulates scientific activity among peers.

- Children's experiences and ideas are more easily recorded for future reference when they put words to their actions.

- In addition to the ways they benefit science learning, conversations build language capacity and promote early literacy.

b. For a few minutes, allow teachers to share successful strategies for facilitating science talks, as well as issues they have encountered. Use the posters you have made to record their comments and ideas. As they share, ask some questions, "Why do you say that strategy worked? What is the evidence of its success? How did it promote science inquiry and learning? How did the children respond?" Try to address the issues during the workshop.

2. **Provide a framework for further discussion of conversations** (15 minutes) using overheads 14.1–14.3. Start with important aspects of conversations that are science focused. Then introduce the idea that there are strategies to avoid. Finally, introduce the settings in which science conversations can occur.

Overhead 14.1: Focus on Science Concepts by Promoting Inquiry

- **Responses that promote reflection**

  - *Restate or paraphrase a child's statement*

  - *Ask children for descriptions about what they did to speed the flow of water, or move it to a lower container*

  - *Wonder with children about what is happening ("I wonder why the water went there?")*

  - *Accept their ideas without judgment and ask the next question ("Why do you think that happened?")*

Teachers can encourage children's reflection by listening carefully and restating without judgment. Teachers can also communicate that they value children's ideas by giving nonverbal cues such as head nods and verbal acknowledgments such as, "That's an interesting idea."

- **Responses that promote analysis**

  - *Ask for descriptive details.*

  - *Ask for examples, comparisons, and alternatives.*

  - *Ask, What if . . . ? Why do you think so? How do you know?*

Describing their observations sets the stage for analysis. When teachers ask why or how, they are probing for the evidence that underlies children's ideas.

OVERHEAD 14.2: RESPONSES THAT INHIBIT OR LIMIT THINKING

- **Responses that inhibit children's thinking**

    – *Explaining the phenomenon to the children*

    – *Cutting children off*

    – *Correcting or telling children what to think*

These are all common responses that teachers have been using for years. They will need to listen to themselves and work to replace these responses with some that encourage thinking.

- **Responses that limit children's thinking**

    – *Lead them to "correct" answer*

    – *Tell them what to do*

    – *Move on too quickly*

Teachers often respond using the "strategies" above, particularly the last one. It takes time to think, and we need to give children time before probing for further responses. This means waiting for responses from many in the group rather than going with the first raised hand or called-out response.

OVERHEAD 14.3: SETTINGS FOR SCIENCE CONVERSATIONS

- **Talks with small groups**
  This is an especially important strategy because small group science talks can involve everyone. This setting can be used to reflect on a water experience, what was learned and what it might mean, or to encourage collaborative problem solving and learning from others.

- **Science talks with the whole group**
  Whole group science talks help children learn from others. Hearing what others have seen and done can help children reflect on their observations, while focusing their attention on the properties of water. Data from multiple experiences can come together and support the analysis process. Various theories will come forward for comparison. New theories may emerge. At the same time, these science talks can give children ideas for how they can engage in future explorations.

- **Talks with materials or documents at the center**
  With both large and small groups, it is important to bring the concrete into the setting. Materials being used in the water centers, photographs, representations, and records of data all help children connect with their investigations.

HELP TEACHERS ANALYZE A SMALL GROUP SCIENCE TALK (25 MINUTES)

PURPOSE: This activity will help participants focus on the role of conversations in deepening children's thinking.

Reinforce ideas by viewing and discussing a small group science talk. Introduce vignette 4 by saying that it was taped in a child care classroom in Connecticut. This vignette was viewed in workshop 7, and it features a group of children engaged in an exploration of sinking and floating. Distribute the workshop 14 vignette observation form and ask that teachers take notes in the vignette 4 column. Also give them the transcript.

After viewing the vignette, ask for teachers' observations, "How did this teacher use the talk to engage the children with inquiry and the science concepts?" Ask for specific examples of strategies and why she may have used them by asking, "What exactly did she say?" "Why do you think she did that?" or "What did that strategy provide for the children?"

Highlight the following points when discussing the vignette:

- The teacher sets the stage for the talk in preceding activities—defines the challenge being investigated in the opening introduction to the activity, connects it to previous explorations, asks for predictions. Setting the activity and science talk up this way engages the children in thinking about the science from the beginning.

- The teacher asks children to share what happened (collecting some data) before asking an analytical question. ("What makes something float?" She might have said, "What do you think makes something float?" in order to show she values the children's ideas.) Analysis is informed by data, and a review of the data prepares children for drawing meaning from it. This conversation would have benefited from a more thorough review of the data. They might have put the items that sank on one plate and the floaters on another and then compared them. How is each group alike?

- The teacher uses the chart they have made and the materials (tubes, objects) to help the children communicate their ideas. Children's memories are aided by seeing these and they can also use them when they do not have words for what they want to say.

- The teacher accepts all ideas that are shared. This is not about what is right or wrong. Her acceptance of all ideas is important to children's inquiry—they will eventually form more sophisticated ideas based on new experiences.

HELP TEACHERS ANALYZE A LARGE GROUP SCIENCE TALK (35 MINUTES)

PURPOSE: This is an opportunity for the teachers to observe a large group science talk. The teacher facilitates a sharing of two children's strategies for investigating water movement.

Support teachers' strategies by viewing and discussing a large group science talk. Introduce vignette 7 by saying that it was taped at a class of four- and five-year-olds in Boston during whole group time. Distribute the transcript and ask teachers to take notes in the vignette 7 column of their observation form.

After viewing the vignette, ask for teachers' observations using the following questions to guide the conversation:

- What science concepts are being explored?

- What aspects of inquiry are these children engaged in? (You may want to refer to the inquiry diagram in the teacher's guide or by showing the overhead.)

- What strategies is the teacher using to deepen science understanding?

- What might she have done differently?

Highlight the following points when discussing the vignette:

- What science concepts are being explored?

  - Both children are exploring the movement of water using a funnel and tube. They have found that the tube contains the water and that when pointed down the water flows down.

- What aspects of inquiry are these children engaged in?

  - They have recorded their experience and are using language to share what they did with classmates. Note the scaffolding the teacher is doing of this process. Ralf has little language, but has done a fairly detailed drawing of his setup and is offered the opportunity to demonstrate what he did. Priya has more language and is less dependent on her representation, which is less detailed.

- What strategies is the teacher using to deepen science understanding?

  – Facilitates a sharing of two children's work.

  – Uses representation, props, and demonstration to support the sharing.

  – Encourages reasoning: "How do you think that one helps to make this one so it doesn't fall?" "Why do you think it might fall down?"

  – Asks question to draw out details: "And then what happened?" "And what did you use this for?" "So was the tube curved like this?"

  – Asks the class if they have tried what Ralf did, getting them to connect the sharing to their own experiences.

  – Asks what Priya found out. This is a good question to begin the process of making meaning of experiences.

- What might she have done differently?

  – Elicited more class participation around the question of similar experiences to Ralf's. For children who said they had done it, she might have asked if they found that water behaved the same way as Ralf's and had a few others speak about their experience.

  – At some point she might have wondered if there was a reason they held the tube down and if they had tried it in another position. She might have wondered how the water would move if the end of the tube was held up. This could have led to the sharing of some experiences, or it might have been the beginning of a new investigation.

- Other points to make:

  – Another important goal is to get children to talk to one another. Encourage children to direct questions and comments to their peers when appropriate.

  – These conversations are hard to manage. Start with brief conversations and extend the length as children build their ability to attend. Use questions and comments to draw in children who may be getting restless.

To conclude, pass out the strategies handout and let teachers know about the next workshop, and give them any assignment you want them to do.

Suggested Next Steps

Conducting science talks is a difficult skill for teachers to learn. It will be helpful if you can give them more support as they incorporate science talks into their practice.

- Both workshops on representation have examples of conversations with children that would help teachers build their skills in this area.

- Guided discussions are an excellent way to deepen teacher understanding of science talks. During these discussions, teachers can share video- or audiotape conversations from their classrooms and discuss them. Transcribing is time consuming, but it is a very effective form of documentation for these kinds of conversations.

- Mentoring is another excellent way to support teachers. Observe a conversation, document it, and then talk with the teacher about what she did, reinforcing the strategies she is using and brainstorming ideas for the missed opportunities.

TRANSCRIPT OF VIDEO VIGNETTE 7:
TALKING ABOUT MOVING WATER

Scene: With teacher guidance, two children are sharing their approaches to moving water through tubes and what they noticed with the class.

The children: Ralf and Priya

Teacher: Can everybody see his picture?

Class: Yes.

Teacher: Okay. So, we have our little funnel, and we have the tube, right? What is this part? Is this part of anything? I'm not sure what that is.

Ralf: That's the part of the water table.

Teacher: Oh, this is the water table?

Ralf: And that's the cup of the water table.

Teacher: So, you need this cup?

Ralf: It was this.

Teacher: You need this cup? And we had these two things, and then what happened? Show me what happened.

Ralf: I poured water in there, and it went down in this leg down here.

Teacher: In this leg? And then what happened? And what did you use this for?

Ralf: To pour it in.

Teacher: Ah, so maybe you could show us what you did.

Ralf: Okay.

Teacher: I'll hold this. So, you got the water, and you put it in there, and then what?

Ralf: I poured in (there), and it went down.

Teacher: So, was the tube curved like this?

Ralf: No.

Teacher: How did it—can you make the tube the way it was? Can you bend the tube so I can . . . We'll just pretend this is the water table on my lap. Did it stay like this? Or did you have to move it for the water to go down in there?

Ralf: I moved it over there.

Teacher: You needed to move it. Okay. Has anybody tried this before?

Class: I did.

Class: No.

Teacher: Priya, can you come up and share your drawing? Thank you, Ralf. *(To Priya as they set up)* I'm sorry.

Priya: I took . . . I took one of the tubes, and then I put it under the cup.

Teacher: You want me to hold this up? Put this up?

Priya: And then I put it under the cup, and I put this on the end of it, and then I poured water into here.

Child: That's—that's like what Tiani did.

Teacher: So, was the funnel like this?

Priya: No. This was straight up.

Teacher: So, turn it this way? And then what? And then the tube needs to go like this?

Priya: Yes. And I poured water through there, and it came in there.

Teacher: So, what happened to the water?

Priya: Well, I poured the water in here, and then it came all the way through here, and went into the cup.

Teacher: So, what did you find out when you did all of this? What did you find out?

Priya: That if you, like . . . if you put it up . . . I mean, if you like put it like different . . . if you put it like over there, it would like come out of there, but . . .

Teacher: If you put it over here, you mean?

Priya: No. If you put the tube over here on this side.

Teacher: Okay. So, put the tube over here . . . yes.

Priya: Over there.

Teacher: Yes.

Priya: But if you put it over there it will come out on that side.

Teacher: Okay. I don't understand what you mean, Priya.

Priya: If you put the water on . . . if you put the . . . if you put the tube on . . . right here, it will come out here.

Teacher: Right.

Priya: You put the tube over here, it will come out over there.

Teacher: So, if you put the tube on this side of the cup, it will come out on this side?

Priya: Yes.

Teacher: But does the water go all the way on the bottom, or just over here on this side?

Priya: All the way on the bottom, and it comes . . . most of it goes on that side.

Teacher: Oh, most of it goes on that side. I see.

Priya: But that's what.

Teacher: And is that what . . . are we looking at this picture, or this picture. I'm not sure which picture we're supposed to be looking at. That one?

Priya: Yes. Because this is the filter, and then this is the water coming through.

Teacher: Oh, that's the water coming through? Okay. All right. Thank you, Priya.

(The children applaud.)

ADVANCED WORKSHOP 14: VIGNETTE OBSERVATION FORM

Note your observations by identifying the teacher strategies and child responses for each vignette in the appropriate column.

Vignette 4	Vignette 7

STRATEGIES FOR FACILITATING SCIENCE TALKS

1. Start slowly. For example, you might begin with five- to ten-minute conversations and increase the time as children increase their engagement. Take cues from the children to decide when to stop and when to continue.

2. Choose a concrete stimulus for the conversation. For example, you might choose materials being used to explore water, such as tubing and a funnel, a child's drawing, or a picture from a book.

3. Be enthusiastic and curious. For example, "I am so excited about what happened this morning. Who wants to talk about the setup on the wire wall?"

4. Model ways of sharing your thoughts and some of the questions you have. For example, "I noticed the water flowed fast when Jasmine held the tube up high. I wonder what happens when it is lower?"

5. Expand on children's observations and ideas. For example, if Kabir says, "It came out here (pointing)," you might rephrase by saying, "Kabir noticed the water coming out of the other end of the hose into the bucket."

6. Ask questions to engage children in analysis. For example, "How are the drops on aluminum foil different from the drops on the paper towel? Why do you think that is? What do you think drops would look like on waxed paper?"

7. Ask questions to help children predict. For example, before going on a walkabout to explore the building, ask, "Where do you think we will find water? What will it look like?" Be sure to follow up by asking why they think so or by getting them to compare different responses.

8. Provide children with the support they need to share their thoughts about the following:
   - Give children time to think before you expect them to respond. Silent time is okay.
   - Find ways for children with limited language and second language learners to demonstrate what they know.
   - Model using descriptive language by explaining a child's actions. For example, "Shannon is showing us how she held the hose to get the water to move fast. She shows how she held it up high."

9. Draw out ideas. For example, "Tuan described using a baster to get water to move up. Has anyone used a different strategy to get water to move up? How did you do it? Does anyone have other ideas they would like to try?"

10. Avoid comments that inhibit or limit thinking. Avoid the following:
    - Explaining the science phenomena yourself
    - Correcting children
    - Leading them to the "correct" answer
    - Moving on too quickly

READ AND REFLECT 14

In preparation for advanced workshop 14, review "The Teacher's Role" (p. 97 in the resources section of the teacher's guide). This section provides advice for facilitating science talks. Find guidance for conducting science talks in the open exploration or focused exploration sections of the guide. Note ideas from the guide that you would like to try below. Facilitate a few small and large group science talks using suggestions from your reading. Note the children's engagement and participation, and complete the reflection questions below. You may want to record a few conversations on audiotape for later reflection.

1. Ideas to try:

2. Successful strategies:

3. Difficulties:

Making and Using Documentation Panels

AT A GLANCE

Purpose:

- Learn about the role documentation panels play in science explorations
- Learn to make and evaluate panels
- Learn to use panels to help children revisit, reflect on, and extend their work

Activity	Time: 1½ hours	Materials
Introduce documentation panels Present an overview of the "what" and "why" of documentation panels. Guide teachers as they examine a sample panel.	30 minutes	• Overhead projector, screen, and overheads 1.2, 1.3, and 15.1–15.5 • Copies of overhead 15.1
Help teachers make documentation panels Support teachers as they use documents they have brought from their classrooms to make panels that illustrate a recent science exploration. Ask them to use the criteria to evaluate their own panels and share their learning.	1 hour	• Overhead projector, screen, and overhead 15.6 • Poster-making supplies • Copies of documentation panel feedback form

Pre-assignment: Read "Guidelines for Creating Documentation Panels" in the teacher's guide (p. 115). Complete workshop 15 assignment.

Advanced Workshop 15: Making and Using Documentation Panels

OBJECTIVES

- Learn about the role documentation panels have in science exploration
- Learn to make and evaluate panels
- Learn to use panels to help children revisit, reflect on, and extend their work

OVERVIEW

- Introduce documentation panels (30 minutes)
- Help teachers make documentation panels (1 hour)

INSTRUCTOR PREPARATION

- **DISTRIBUTE ASSIGNMENT.** At least a week before the workshop, give teachers the workshop 15 assignment. Also, tell teachers to read the guidelines for creating documentation panels in the teacher's guide.

MATERIALS

- Overhead projector, screen, and overheads 1.2, 1.3, and 15.1–15.6
- Poster-making supplies, including oak tag, rubber cement, markers, assorted colored paper, scissors
- Copies of handouts: documentation panel feedback form and workshop 15 assignment
- Copies of overhead 15.1 for small groups

Activity

INTRODUCTION TO DOCUMENTATION PANELS (30 MINUTES)

PURPOSE: This discussion provides the essential information about panels—what are they, why they are important, and how to use them.

1. **INTRODUCE THE WORKSHOP** (5 minutes) by telling teachers they will be focusing on a practical skill for the next hour and a half—making documentation panels. At the same time, teachers will see how this process triggers valuable ideas about their work. Confirm that everyone has brought documents for making panels. Pair anyone who did not bring documents with someone who did.

2. **PROVIDE AN OVERVIEW OF THE VALUE OF PANELS** (20 minutes). Connect panels to science learning by showing and discussing the following overhead sequence:

a. Remind teachers of the science goals by reviewing overheads 1.2 and 1.3 and by referring them to the outcomes in the teacher's guide on p. 120. Tell teachers that the main goal of documentation panels is to make the science learning visible. Highlighting children's engagement with science processes and ideas is key.

b. Ask teachers to form groups of three. Give each group a copy of overhead 15.1. Read the panel text from the box below.

> The title of this documentation panel is, "What works best for making water go UP through the hose?"
>
> The text on Chidemma's drawing says, "The yellow water went up from the bucket on the floor in the hose."
>
> Patrick's quote to the left of his drawing says, "I try to put the hose in the water and then it went in the other table. The water went down in the hose. The green cover worked good. And the pump."

Show overhead 15.2, and review the questions they will use to guide their discussion. Leave the overhead up while they talk.

OVERHEAD 15.2: DOCUMENTATION PANEL DISCUSSION QUESTIONS

- **What is the intended message in this panel? What is the teacher trying to communicate?**
  Look for ideas such as the teacher wanted to show the children's process of inquiry and the learning that came from it. She has used two children's representations and their descriptions of their process. Drawings of materials used are combined with children's votes on the effectiveness of each.

- **Where is the science engagement and learning in this panel?**
  This panel illustrates a focused investigation of water flow. Children are exploring the kinds and amount of force that needs to be used to move water up through a hose in order to counter the pull of gravity that results in a downward flow. They have experimented with different materials, observed the results, represented their experience, and discussed the data, drawing conclusions about the relative effectiveness of the different materials used.

- **How well are these messages communicated? Where is the evidence of children's science learning?**
  Look for ideas such as the use of photos, drawings, and captions to convey the inquiry process and reflect the children's science ideas. The title is important to understanding what is happening. The children's work adds authenticity that would not be there without this evidence of the children's engagement.

- **How would you change this panel?**
  While the panel shows the inquiry process, it does not explain what the children learned about water. The data that lead to determining the effectiveness of each material is not included—an important aspect of inquiry. How did they determine that the baster was not so good? Also, there is no indication of what Chidemma did to move the water up. It would not move up on its own, and Chidemma's actions are an important learning that should be shared.

---

c. After ten minutes, show overhead 15.1 and discuss teachers' responses to each question. Look for ideas like those above in the overhead box.

If you have time, show overhead 15.3: "Michael's Panel." This is a panel that illustrates the work of one child who has played a role in creating his panel (making the collage portion). Again, read the text of the panel.

The paragraph at the bottom right-hand corner of the photo is a quote from Michael. It reads, "I had to scoop water up, dump in the funnel—went down squirted out like an elephant. I had to go quick, so it wouldn't ooze out, so it would keep coming out fast, fast, fast. Keep going far, far, far."

Captions along the collage read:

Hand holding the handle, pouring the water out, into the big funnel, hand holding the funnel so the funnel wouldn't fall off the tube, tube squirting water from the inside of the tub, small funnel hole on the end, shot up like an airplane going up or an elephant shooting up.

Use the questions on overhead 15.2 to discuss teachers' reactions.

Look for ideas like these:

- What is the intended message in this panel?
  This panel shows Michael's exploration of water flow.

- Where is the science engagement and learning in this panel?
  Michael is learning about how to regulate the speed of water when pouring it into a hose. Clearly he wants fast-moving water and has found a way to achieve that. Michael has explored water flow with a focus on speed, observed the effect of his efforts, and represented his experience using yarn to represent the water and other collage materials to represent the tubing. There is also a drawing he did. He has shared his experience by describing the process and descriptively explaining what he learned.

- How well are these messages communicated?
  The combination of photos, collage, drawing, and text give an accurate picture of Michael's experience.

- How would you change this panel?
  This question allows teachers a chance to think critically. If they have ideas, get them to share how their idea improves the communication of Michael's understanding of the science or engagement in inquiry.

3. **ASK TEACHERS HOW THEY WOULD DESCRIBE A DOCUMENTATION PANEL** (5 minutes). You might ask: "How might we define *documentation panel?*" Discuss a few ideas, then show and review overhead 15.4.

OVERHEAD 15.4: WHAT IS A SCIENCE FOCUSED-DOCUMENTATION PANEL?

- **A poster that illustrates science inquiry and learning**
  Share that the real benefit of documentation panels is that they make the process of inquiry and learning visible to teachers, children, and families.

- **A multimedia presentation**
  Explain that a combination of text, photos, and work samples can capture the complexity of the process in which children are engaged. As teachers learn to create panels they will also learn to evaluate the quality of each document they use—which photos actually illustrate engagement and science learning, which representations reveal science understandings, and which quotes from the children communicate important science ideas. Over time, teachers' understanding of science and children's learning deepen as they repeatedly engage in this process.

- **A story that can either take place over time or at one point in time**
  Mention that documentation panels can illustrate one activity or a sequence of activities. Panels that have a narrow focus are more useful in working with the children, but panels that span a longer period of time can help teachers evaluate their teaching. Then, they can look for connections from one activity to the next.

4. REVIEW THE USES OF DOCUMENTATION PANELS (5 minutes) by asking teachers how they might use them. After listening to their ideas for a few minutes, show overhead 15.5.

OVERHEAD 15.5: USES OF DOCUMENTATION PANELS

- **A stimulus for science talks**
  The documentation panel helps children share what they have done with others. It can also be posted in the room for all of the children to refer to as they move forward in their exploration.

- **An opportunity to promote literacy as well as science**
  Children are eager to "read" their own stories and will learn a lot from the process of "reading" panels.

- **Educate families**
  Panels on display provide families with insights into what children are doing and the science they are learning. Keep families and your colleagues in mind as potential audiences for documentation panels.

- **Teacher reflection**
  The process of making the panel is a valuable opportunity for teachers to reflect on their work and consider next steps to take with these children and the whole group.

HELPING TEACHERS MAKE DOCUMENTATION PANELS (1 HOUR)

PURPOSE: This activity allows participants to reflect on the science teaching and learning in their classroom as they learn to create a panel that they can use with children and families.

1. **INTRODUCE THE ACTIVITY** (10 minutes) by telling teachers that they will now have a chance to make a panel. Show overhead 15.6 as a review.

OVERHEAD 15.6: MAKING DOCUMENTATION PANELS

- **Identify a science exploration focus to illustrate**
  Keep science concept(s) and inquiry skill(s) at the forefront of your message. You might focus on ideas children have about drops—predictions and what they actually found, or strategies for moving water from one container to another, the results of a challenge, data collected, ideas generated by comparing data (such as the length of flow from different holes).

- **Collect documents that will help tell your story**
  Collect work samples, photographs, dialogue, and observational notes that tell the story.

- **Arrange documents on posterboard**
  Arrange documents left to right and in chronological order. When you are satisfied with the arrangement, glue them down and add captions.

- **Add a title that focuses on your readers**
  Be sure your title communicates your key message.

Review the available materials (oak tag, rubber cement, markers, and so on). Tell teachers that their task is to organize a presentation of the documents they have brought. Remind them to add captions that explain what is shown in the photos and work samples.

Suggest they open their teacher's guides to the science outcomes chart. Tell teachers that they can use this chart to highlight how children used the inquiry skills or explored different science concepts.

> **Instructor's Notes**
>
> Watch out! Creating documentation panels is sometimes considered an appropriate place for teacher decorations. You may need to remind some that this is about science learning and that decorations can detract from the important message about the children's engagement and learning.

Allow twenty-five minutes to lay out panels.

2. **SUPPORT THEIR WORK** (25 minutes) by wandering around the room. Answer questions and listen to their discussion to be sure they are on track and moving ahead.

3. **ASK THEM TO USE THE CRITERIA** (15 minutes) on the documentation panel feedback form to evaluate their own panel. Pass out the forms and let teachers know that they can continue to work on their panel. However, while they are working, they should consider how well their panel meets the criteria. Join in these discussions as you move around the room, sharing your own thoughts. Let them know when you will bring them together. It is not essential that they finish their panels—they can always do it after the workshop. If some finish early, encourage them to wander around and look at what others have done.

4. **BRING THEM TOGETHER FOR FINAL COMMENTS** after 10 minutes. Ask a few groups to comment on particular decisions they made that highlight the process and the different approaches they have taken. You might want to ask what they learned from considering the criteria and what they would do differently next time. Other possible discussion questions might include the following:

    -   Which inquiry skill(s) did you decide to focus on? Why? How did you decide on the concept?

    -   While making your panel, what have you learned about science teaching and learning? Keep teachers focused on their own panel and what they might have learned about the children or their own teaching as they reflected on the documents.

    -   What did you learn by looking at other panels? Again, keep the focus on children's engagement and learning and on the teacher's role. If teachers have obviously benefited by sharing their work, encourage them to think about how they can continue to do this. Suggest that in addition to sharing panels, they can also share and discuss photographs, children's work samples, or audiotaped conversations.

    -   How might you use this panel with your children? Ask, "What do you hope the children will gain?" Look for ideas such as, "I would take the panel to a science talk to help children share what they did with the others, and I would post it in the room so others can refer to it." Such activities can stimulate children's thinking and help them revisit and build on their ideas and experiences, as well as those of others.

In closing, encourage teachers to share their panels and to use them with children and families. Remind them when and where the next workshop or study group is and what they need to do to prepare.

Suggested Next Steps

- Follow up with teachers, asking how they are using panels in their classrooms. Have they displayed them at children's eye level? Did they use them to encourage a science talk? How did it go?

- Offer workshop 14: "Facilitating Science Talks" or workshop 13: "Using Children's Representations as Teaching Tools," which will give teachers ideas about how to use the panels to stimulate conversations.

- Focus a few guided discussions on the use of panels with children, allowing teachers to share and analyze their experiences.

- Offer to help teachers who are interested in forming a documentation panel group. Supply a space, supplies, and tools for them to use when they get together to make panels.

DOCUMENTATION PANEL FEEDBACK FORM

Name: _____

Panel: _____

Use the following criteria as you consider the panel's effectiveness:

- Is the science content, with which the children were engaged, evident? What is it? Where is the evidence?

- Is children's inquiry process evident? What is it? Where is the evidence?

- Does the panel provide important background information? Do you understand what you need to know about the setting, timing, and what the children were doing?

- How well do photographs capture children's engagement and actions?

- How well do the work samples and quotes illustrate the important message about science engagement and learning?

- One thing that is really good about this panel:

- One suggestion for improvement:

Advanced Workshop 15 Assignment

1. Read the section about documentation panels on p. 115 in the teacher's guide. Review the curriculum and look for places where the directions ask you to make a documentation panel.

2. Identify an aspect of your children's exploration that you would like to document.

3. Collect a set of three or four documents that you can use to create a panel that reflects your children's engagement in science inquiry. Use the following guidelines when collecting:
   - Documents should all be related to a particular aspect of your exploration. For example, they might be about strategies for moving water or an investigation of drops.
   - The documents should be varied, including some or all of the following: children's drawings or paintings, photos of three-dimensional representations, photos of children engaged in the exploration, quotes from their conversation, predictions, and conclusions.

The Culture of Inquiry

- An emphasis on the importance of exploring water

- An emphasis on inquiry

- Sharing observations and ideas

- Recording observations and experiences

The Science Teacher's Goals

- Encourage children to explore water

- Guide children's inquiry

- Deepen children's science understanding

SCIENCE TEACHING AND LEARNING

- Young children develop ideas about science from their life experiences.

- New experiences lead children to challenge previous naïve ideas.

- A balance between exploration and thinking, reasoning, and theorizing provides a strong basis for learning.

- Inquiry that leads to science learning takes time.

- When guided, children have the ability to engage in all aspects of the inquiry process.

Key Ideas about This Approach to Science Learning

- Building understanding of important science concepts is an appropriate goal for young children.

- Children naturally form ideas about the world based on their life experiences.

- In inquiry-based science it is important for teachers to provide new experiences that can lead children to more sophisticated theories.

"Experience is not the best teacher.

It sounds like heresy, but when you think about it, it's

reflection on experience that makes it educational."

—George Forman,

Professor Emeritus, University of Massachusetts

SCIENCE BOOKS AND SCIENCE LEARNING

- Stimulate science inquiry and thinking

- Provide images and examples of careers in science

- Provide information and ideas relevant to children's scientific inquiries

- Connect science exploration with the world outside the classroom

Science Books and Literacy Development

- Build language skills

- Introduce many genres of books about science

- Engage children with print

- Develop a love of books

Uses of Books about Water

- To read aloud and discuss

- To read aloud as introduction to a new idea or challenge

- To look at and talk about

- To encourage descriptive language and representation

Key Elements of Assessment Process

- Collecting data

- Analyzing data regularly

- Drawing conclusions and making decisions

MAKAYLA'S DROPS

drops make circles

puddle with drops

Makayla

ALEX'S RAINDROPS

Alex - rain going down into the puddle.

TZEIDEL'S WATER FLOW

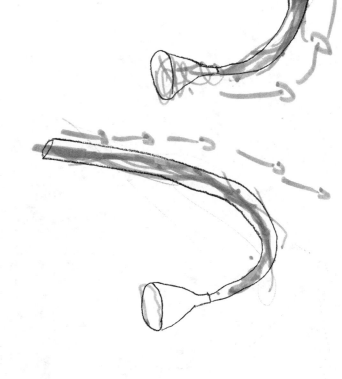

1. no blowing 2. no squirting 3. no pumping

Katherine's Water Flow

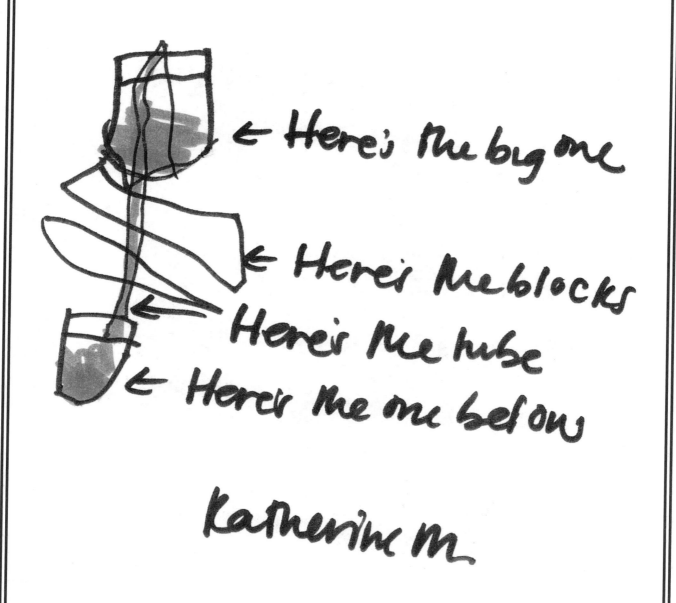

← Here's the big one

← Here's the blocks

← Here's the tube

← Here's the one below

Katherine M.

BETUL'S DROPS

LUCY'S SPINNING DROPS

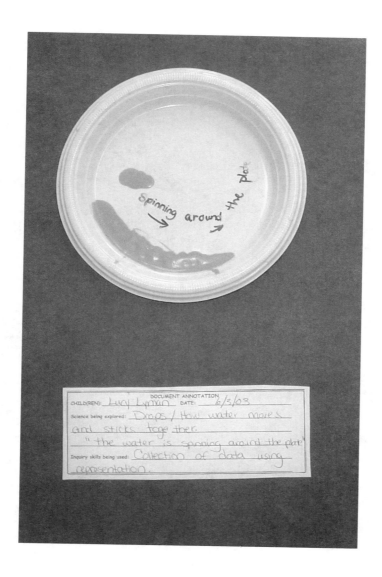

MORE WATER FLOW

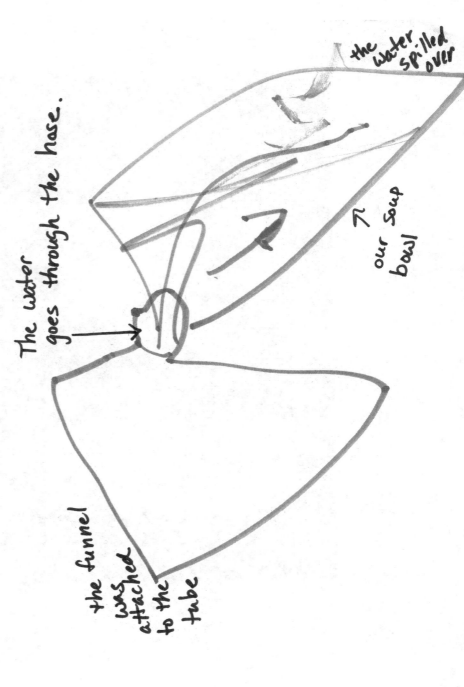

the funnel was attached to the tube

The water goes through the hose.

our soup bowl

the water spilled over

SAMPLE DOCUMENT ANNOTATION

DOCUMENT ANNOTATION

Child(ren): Myles Byrnes   **Date:** 6/3/03

Science being explored: Drops—How water moves and sticks together

Inquiry skills being used: Collection of data using representation

USE REPRESENTATIONS TO DEEPEN LEARNING AND PROMOTE INQUIRY

- Build ability to communicate observations and ideas

- Focus on particular science ideas

- Build a culture of inquiry and collaboration

- Connect children's explorations from one day to the next

- Recap what has been learned at key points in an exploration

- Stimulate discussion in which children synthesize and analyze their work

FOCUS ON SCIENCE CONCEPTS BY PROMOTING INQUIRY

- Responses that promote reflection

- Responses that promote analysis

RESPONSES THAT INHIBIT OR LIMIT THINKING

Responses that inhibit children's thinking:

- explaining

- cutting children off

- correcting children

Responses that limit children's thinking:

- leading children to the correct answer

- telling children what to do

- moving on too quickly

Settings for Science Conversations

- Talks with small groups

- Science talks with the whole group

- Talks with materials or documents at the center

Documentation Panel

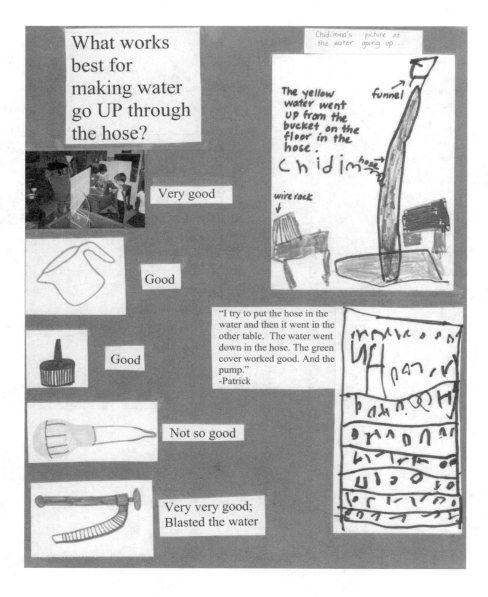

What works best for making water go UP through the hose?

Very good

Good

Good

Not so good

Very very good; Blasted the water

Chidimma's picture of the water going up...

The yellow water went up from the bucket on the floor in the hose.

Chidim

funnel

hose

wire rack

"I try to put the hose in the water and then it went in the other table. The water went down in the hose. The green cover worked good. And the pump."
-Patrick

Documentation Panel Discussion Questions

- What is the intended message in this panel?
  What is the teacher trying to communicate?

- Where is the science engagement and learning in this panel?

- How well are these messages communicated?
  Where is the evidence of children's science learning?

- How would you change this panel?

Michael's Panel

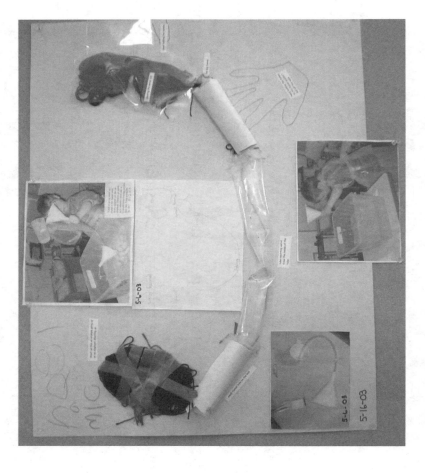

What Is a Science-Focused Documentation Panel?

- A poster that illustrates science inquiry and learning

- A multimedia presentation

- A story that can either take place over time or at one point in time

Uses of Documentation Panels

- A stimulus for science talks

- An opportunity to promote literacy as well as science

- Educate families

- Teacher reflection

Making Documentation Panels

- Identify a science exploration focus to illustrate

- Collect documents that will help tell your story

- Arrange documents on posterboard

- Add a title that focuses your readers

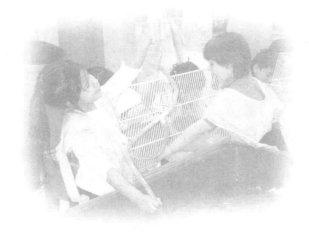

guided discussions

Whether teachers are just beginning to use *Exploring Water with Young Children* or are refining their practices as science teachers, you can use guided discussions to provide ongoing support and build collaboration. Through group analysis of various materials, such as video from classrooms or children's work samples, teachers build a deeper understanding of the science teaching and learning in their classrooms. By provoking questions and reflection, guided discussions support teachers as they engage in the ongoing process of refining their approach to teaching science. Guided discussions have the following advantages:

- **IMPROVE SCIENCE TEACHING AND LEARNING**
  These analytical discussions help teachers understand their role as science teachers and develop appropriate expectations for their children. Over time they develop a better understanding of the connections between their teaching and children's science learning. Improved practice is reinforced by child engagement and learning.

- **CREATE A COMMUNITY OF ADULT LEARNERS**
  Working in isolation, teachers often feel overwhelmed and very alone. By providing time and creating a structure for collaboration, you can help teachers share their resources and energy, while gaining a greater sense of community. This kind of support system encourages teachers to try out new ideas, share their experiences, and learn from others.

Once they have participated in the basic workshops, the guided discussions will keep enthusiasm alive, while supporting the implementation of *Exploring Water with Young Children* in each teacher's classroom. Guided discussions have some common elements, which include the following:

- A group of teachers who are motivated to explore the approach found in *Exploring Water with Young Children* and to talk about how it relates to their practice and to children's learning

- A leader who has identified learning objectives and is willing to commit to the group and its development

- Documentation from teachers' classrooms (including video clips or observations of teaching practice, child work samples, or audiotaped conversations) to serve as common discussion points in group meetings

- A set of questions designed to guide the discussion, build connections between this approach and the documentation being used, help teachers reflect on their practice, and develop ways to apply new ideas to their work

Your guided discussions will be most successful under the following conditions:

- Discussions involve a small group of teachers (four to seven is optimal)
- Attendance is seen as part of teachers' regular responsibilities
- Time—an hour or hour and a half—is set aside regularly (at least monthly) for the discussions
- Discussions have a focus on practical aspects of science teaching and are structured so one builds on another
- A supervisor, mentor teacher, or other program leader is committed to planning and facilitating all of the discussions
- Leadership within the group is cultivated and the group becomes more self-sustaining

Selecting the right time to introduce guided discussions is also key to their effectiveness. They can be introduced at several points:

- **AFTER THE BASIC WORKSHOPS.** If you are working with a small group of teachers and want to move to a more informal setting after the basic workshops, consider starting guided discussions. Teachers will probably benefit from continual examination of the teacher's guide if they can focus on the stage of the exploration where they are currently working, either open exploration or focused exploration. Rereading sections of the teacher's guide, reviewing vignettes and work samples from the basic workshops, and sharing observations from their classroom will help them as they translate the print curriculum into their daily classroom life.

- **AFTER EACH ADVANCED WORKSHOP.** Guided discussions might also be offered in between the workshops with a specific focus on the teacher's application of the content from the workshop. In this approach, ongoing guided discussions are interrupted by workshops that provide new content. For example, if participants explored deepening children's science understanding in their last workshop, they might view a videotape from one of their classrooms, analyzing the children's engagement and considering possible next steps. Or they might read and discuss one of the articles recommended in the "Next Steps" box. One or two teachers can be responsible for sharing their classroom experience in each guided discussion. Stay on a topic for as many sessions as it takes for each teacher to discuss her work. Over time, teachers will begin to take some responsibility for planning the discussions. They will select topics, provide stimulus material, and plan discussion questions. They might select a focus that relates to their role as a facilitator of inquiry, such as encouraging representation or guiding science talks. Or they may want to better understand how to assess different kinds of child work by developing their observation skills or jointly examining work samples and transcripts.

Preparing for Guided Discussions

A successful guided discussion begins with thoughtful preparation. You will want to start by identifying teachers' needs and then determining appropriate goals, materials, and questions. For teachers who have participated only in the basic workshops, these discussions can provide a more in-depth look at the teacher's guide, a more thorough discussion of some of the video vignettes and work samples used in the basic workshops, and time to explore emerging issues on documenting children's work. Try not to let the focus shift to control issues in the classroom. These group discussions are about the teaching and learning of science. Remind teachers of this and suggest another forum for the other topics they bring up.

Teachers who have participated in the advanced workshops can examine their own documents, which will stimulate and guide their reflection as they adopt new approaches and will provide a vehicle for ongoing support and collaboration.

Use the "Sample Guided Discussion Plans" in "Resources" (p. 198) when you begin to prepare your meetings. These sample plans provide goals, recommended materials, and discussion questions for three different kinds of discussions. Copy and use the planning form to record your plans and reflections for each discussion.

Use the following guidance to ensure the success of your discussions.

ASSESS TEACHERS' NEEDS

As you plan when and how to use guided discussions, you will need to take into consideration the teachers' backgrounds with curriculum and science teaching and the amount of previous experience they have had with *Exploring Water with Young Children*. Some teachers may have a background in science, or your program might be using a curriculum that embraces the same teaching approaches. These teachers might grasp the approach to science and science teaching more quickly, and they might be ready to share more sophisticated insights and their own experiences in a self-directed setting. Teachers without this background will need a more intensive introduction to the teacher's guide first. Use the "Science Teacher Development Stages" in the section on assessing teacher growth (p. 203) to determine appropriate goals for teachers.

An essential aspect of their work as science teachers will be elevating the science content in the children's explorations. The teachers must have some understanding and experience with these science concepts in order to recognize them in their children's work. After their hands-on experiences with these concepts in the basic workshops, the guided discussions are a great place to reinforce what teachers understand. Always talk about the science that is present in the documents being discussed, the concepts they are exploring, and what they understand.

It is also important to consider teachers' own perceptions of their needs. As you conduct the workshops, listen carefully to their questions and concerns. Provide opportunities for them to suggest topics they want to focus on. If they have particular interests, their motivation to participate will be high.

DEVELOP A GOAL THAT RESPONDS TO TEACHERS' NEEDS

A goal is stated in broad terms and reflects one aspect of the approach found in *Exploring Water with Young Children* (such as to better understand how children use representation to deepen their understanding of science ideas). Use the "Science Teacher Development Stages" on p. 203 as you think about appropriate goals for teachers. Also remember to take their interests into consideration. It will probably take several guided discussion meetings to fully explore one goal, as there will often be multiple perspectives to explore and you will want each teacher to have time to discuss her classroom.

DEVELOP LEARNING OBJECTIVES FOR EACH GOAL

Learning objectives provide more specificity than the goal. That is, objectives elucidate the goal by articulating the major points that you want teachers to take away from the discussion. Each goal might have several objectives. For example, if your goal is to better understand why representation is important to science learning, three objectives might be the following:

(1) recognizing children's science ideas in their representations, (2) understanding the relationship between media being used (drawing, clay, three-dimensional collage) and the qualities of children's representations, and (3) exploring the role the teacher can play in encouraging representation and using it to deepen learning. It is the objectives that will determine the content focus, the appropriate materials to use, and your guiding questions.

Select Materials

Select material that will illustrate the learning objectives and fuel discussion. Whether you select a video clip, a section of the teacher's guide, children's work samples, or a reading recommended in the bibliography, the resource you select should achieve the following:

- Challenge teachers' previous notions about science teaching and learning (These types of resources are more likely to provoke discussion than information that confirms what teachers already know.)

- Clearly illustrate children's engagement and science understandings, as well as the learning objective you have developed

- If using a video, feature a situation that represents an aspect of the *Exploring Water with Young Children* curriculum

- If using a reading or case study, select one that contains relevant content written at a level appropriate for the teachers in the group

As you prepare, become thoroughly familiar with the material. Consider the main message that the document conveys, how these ideas compare with teachers' current thoughts or practices, and how different teachers might respond.

Develop Discussion Questions

Develop discussion questions that will stimulate analysis of key points and practices. Create a core group of questions and a set of subquestions to raise if central points are missed during the discussion. Identify questions that will guide the discussion carefully from being descriptive to being analytical by following these four steps:

1. **Begin with general open-ended questions** about the document (such as, "What did you think about the article we read?").

2. **Ask for objective description of the material** (such as, "What do you see in this work sample? How would you describe its key features?"). Or you might ask teachers to take observational notes when watching a videotape and then review what they saw.

3. **Ask teachers to draw inferences,** analyzing what they have seen by making connections between the stimulus and the content ideas (such as, "What exactly did this teacher do to encourage the conversation? What was the connection between the teacher's actions and the children's engagement? Did you see missed opportunities? What might you have done differently?"). Always include some discussion of the children's science knowledge to reinforce the teachers' attention to the science concepts.

4. **Finally, ask them to draw conclusions,** making connections to their own teaching (such as, "What connections can you make to the work you are doing in your classroom? Which of the approaches used here might work with your children? Which ideas generated by the group are worth trying?").

HELP PARTICIPANTS PREPARE FOR THE DISCUSSION

The teachers in your guided discussions can also prepare. You can help them by doing the following:

- Provide teachers with information about the content you will focus on beforehand to promote more thoughtful reflection. (For example, you might want them to read a portion of the teacher's guide or a related article or book chapter.)

- Share discussion questions, if you have them prepared.

Leading Guided Discussions

LAY THE GROUNDWORK IN THE FIRST MEETING

At your first meeting, spend some time as a group establishing the ground rules. Agree on a time limit and times to meet—keep in mind that regularly scheduled discussions have maximum impact. Ensure that the group knows that they are to listen respectfully to what others are saying and not interrupt. And let teachers know that a successful discussion depends more on what they have to say than on what you say. Rather, your role is to stimulate the discussion, keep the focus on science, summarize the group's thinking, and create bridges to the next level of questions.

FOLLOW THIS THREE-PHASE PROCESS WHEN FACILITATING GROUP MEETINGS

PHASE 1: Open the meeting by briefly describing the content that is the focus for this discussion. For example, you might be examining a particular section of the teacher's guide or an aspect of the teachers' role. If you asked your teachers to read a section of the guide or a related article before they came, provide time for them to share what they learned from the reading and list their ideas on a chart for later reference. Add to their list any important points that haven't come up yet. Explicit presentation of the relevant teaching and learning content is necessary for thoughtful analysis.

PHASE 2: Introduce and review the materials. Briefly introduce the material and its purpose, connecting it back to the content you have just reviewed. For example, if you are working on developing the ability to engage children in conversations, and teachers will be analyzing a videotape of a science talk, introduce the viewing by asking teachers to focus on the strategies that you have just reviewed with them. Teachers will tune in differently and ask different questions depending on how you focus their attention. If your document is print materials, such as children's drawings or a series of photographs, try to have several sets so everyone can easily review them.

PHASE 3: Guide the discussion using the questions that you developed to help the group fully explore important points. Remember the four steps that guide question development: (1) begin with general open-ended questions, (2) ask for objective descriptions, (3) draw inferences, and (4) draw conclusions. Leave a few minutes to summarize key points by distilling the thoughts and responses of teachers into several key points.

KEEP THE DISCUSSION FOCUSED ON THE TOPIC

Use these tips to promote full participation:

- Listen carefully and monitor teachers' body language to stay aware of how the group is doing. If you are not sure, check in with a simple "How are you doing with the discussion?"

- Ensure that each teacher has a chance to speak. Engage reluctant participants by making eye contact with them and smiling. Let them know through your body language that they have your support when they are ready to speak.

- Discourage anyone from dominating the conversation by moving the question to another person or by saying, "Let's hear from someone else on that issue."

- Encourage teachers to speak and listen to one another, "Marie, you look like you have a suggestion for Joan. Let her know what you are thinking." Some teachers may be tempted to direct their comments to you or to wait for your response.

- Provide time after you ask a question. Teachers need time to reflect and come up with a thoughtful response. Your silence will communicate that it is their turn to talk and that it is all right for them to take time to think.

- Challenge ideas without challenging a teacher personally.

Build Communication and Leadership among Teachers

FOLLOW UP WITH EACH TEACHER

Whether it is individually or in the next discussion, provide time for teachers to talk about how implementing these new ideas went in their classrooms. If you are addressing the same topic over several discussions, you will want to open discussions with some reporting on their successes and issues to set the stage for further dialogue. List issues on a chart and return them at the end to see what new implications might help address issues. If you regularly observe and have conferences with these teachers, these are ideal times to acknowledge the progress they have made and the impact they have on children's learning. At the same time, you can pinpoint ongoing issues that you might want to build into guided discussion goals in the future.

ENCOURAGE TEACHER LEADERSHIP

As your teachers learn the culture and process for engaging in guided discussions, begin to give them responsibility for planning and facilitating.

- Support teachers as they learn to create documents of the teaching and learning in their classrooms. Provide equipment and help with videotaping and photographing. Interested community groups might help by making contributions for equipment or volunteering time to help in the classroom. Be sure teachers have varied materials for children's representation. Give them time to reflect and plan.

- Let teachers plan guided discussion meetings with you. Help them learn the questioning sequence as they use the guided discussion planning form.

- Take a supporting role as you give them responsibility for facilitating meetings. While you let them take the lead, be prepared to jump in if they want support. You might ask a question to redirect a conversation that is getting off track or move the focus from a teacher who is dominating the dialogue.

- Debrief with them after, allowing them to share their feelings and questions. Use the planning form reflection questions to guide the conversation.

promoting teacher growth through mentoring

The basic and advanced workshops and the guided discussions provide an effective social setting for learning about science teaching. Your teachers will also benefit from individual attention that focuses on their own issues as they implement *Exploring Water with Young Children* in their classrooms. A supervisor or mentor can play a critical role in providing this individualized support, helping teachers evaluate their efforts and build their capacity as science teachers.

The primary goal of mentoring is to guide teachers' development as science teachers through reflection on their practice. You will help them choose appropriate goals, document their work, analyze their practice, and modify their approach to science teaching and learning. Mentoring provides important opportunities to build teachers' ability to do the following:

- Understand the science concepts in the context of children's play, conversations, and representations.

- Evaluate the teaching strategies they are using and their impact on children's science engagement and learning.

- Examine documents from their classrooms (videotape, transcripts of conversations, children's work samples, photographs, and observational notes) for evidence of children's inquiry and science understandings, as well as evidence of teaching effectiveness.

- Make informed decisions about their next steps with children's inquiry.

Ideally, mentors understand early childhood development, the complex nature of inquiry-based science, and the science being taught, and are able to analyze classroom science events. Effective mentors serve as guides: they share what they see, their knowledge, and their expertise in an objective and positive manner, while challenging teachers' thoughts and pushing their practice to new levels of competence. A mentor might be a supervisor, a professional developer, or a teacher who has reached the stage of development where they are refining their knowledge.

Observation and conferences are probably the most important tools mentors have for providing individualized support to teachers. Documentation collected during classroom observations provides the basis for collaborative analysis of teaching and learning, as well as for planning the next steps. The mentor's understanding of the specific classroom context, gained through observation, is essential for guiding teacher reflection and self-assessment.

The outcomes of this work will contribute to the successful implementation of *Exploring Water with Young Children*. To conduct effective observations and conferences, follow these four steps:

1. Establish development goals and objectives with each teacher.

2. Prepare for classroom observations.

3. Conduct classroom observations.

4. Discuss the observations.

Step 1: Establish Development Goals and Objectives with Each Teacher

Use the first visit to establish several development goals with each teacher. Select a goal to start with and develop a few specific objectives that will be the focus of the teacher's initial work and your observations. For example, teachers may want to work on their ability to facilitate science talks. Possible objectives might include asking open-ended questions or to continue their exploration from one day to the next. Use the following steps to develop goals that both you and the teacher agree on:

- Conduct an initial classroom observation using "Evaluating Science Teaching" from "Resources" in the teacher's guide. This will guide recording what you see when observing. Review the teacher development stages on p. 203 to help you determine which parts of the form would be most appropriate to use with each teacher.

- Ask the teacher to use the evaluation form to reflect on her teaching and think about her goals.

- Meet with the teacher. Elicit her thoughts and share your observations. Together, determine the goals and specific objectives using the teacher development plan (p. 211). Use one form for each goal.

Step 2: Prepare for Classroom Observations

Successful classroom observations begin with planning. As you arrange for your visits, assure teachers that the goal of these observations is to support their growth as science teachers, not to judge their teaching for a high-stakes evaluation.

- Schedule a time to observe. Arrange a time when the classroom activity is in line with the teacher's current objectives. For example, if the teacher is working on facilitating large group science talks, schedule your visit to gain a full picture of a large group conversation.

- Conduct a pre-observation conversation with the teacher. Whether on-site or on the phone, get some background information to guide your observation. This information will be crucial when you begin to examine the teaching and learning.

Find out the following:

- The teacher's specific goals for children's engagement and learning
- Aspects of inquiry she expects the children to be engaged in
- Teaching strategies she will use to encourage and guide children's inquiry
- What has led up to these particular goals and activities
- The progress she feels she has made and frustrations she might feel in achieving her current goal
- Documentation (videotape, audiotape, or photographs) that might help illustrate this observation, as well as the notes you will take

Step 3: Conduct Classroom Observations

Use these strategies to develop an approach to observation that effectively supports teacher development:

- Check in with the teacher when you arrive. Without disturbing the classroom activity, find out if there have been any changes in the teacher's plans. Unusual circumstances will influence the flow of the day and what you can achieve in your observation.

- Document what you see and hear. It will be important to have specific information from your observation when you have a conference with the teacher. Take careful notes on paper that has been set up with three columns: child behaviors/comments, teacher responses, my thoughts. Separating your objective information into the child and teacher columns will help you make connections between the two later on. The subjective reactions you note in the right-hand column will help you remember the outstanding events when you plan the conference. Photographs (especially in series), video, and audiotapes all provide clear evidence of children's engagement and are excellent supplements to your notes.

- Remain open and friendly. The classroom will function at its best when you are viewed as a friend. While maintaining your focus, engage in brief interactions with the children who are curious about your presence. "I am here because I want to watch you play," is a good response. It shows an interest in the children while letting them know that it is their activity that you are most interested in. Your interactions with children might model a particular strategy or test its effectiveness, or it might help you gain a new understanding of a particular child or dynamic. If there is a difficult situation and an extra pair of hands is needed, pitch in and help. The teacher needs to know that you are there to support her.

Step 4: Discuss the Observation

Timely, objective feedback will play a key role in a teacher's growth over time. Plan the conference soon after the observation. The events of the day will be fresh in your mind and the teacher's if you set the conference for the same day or the next. When you meet, invite the teacher to bring additional documentation of the events you observed. Children's work samples, a documentation panel, class-made book, or a set of photographs can provide an additional lens into the teaching and learning in the classroom.

Many teachers have not had the benefit of individual support that is focused on their professional growth. They will need time to learn how the process works and that they can trust your confidence and intentions, especially if you are their supervisor. Start by letting them control the agenda for the conference. You might set the focus on *Exploring Water with Young Children*. Then let them show you what is happening and talk about their accomplishments and the issues on their mind. Once they have overcome any defensiveness and have learned that you are a helpful resource, you can share your perceptions, ask more challenging questions, and involve them in goal setting.

Once you get under way, keep the science concepts and inquiry process in the foreground as you use the following process to guide the teacher's reflection:

- Reflect on the observation and plan the conference. Take time to prepare for the conference. Think about what you saw and heard in the classroom and about what it means for this teacher's development as a science teacher. In preparation, complete the "Science Teacher Observation Synthesis" form (see "Resources"). Note the highlights of the interactions you observed in the child and teacher column. Select the events that are related to points you want to make or to specific events you want the teacher to think about. Consider the questions and comments that will encourage teacher reflection and problem solving. Note them in the box at the bottom of the form. Take time to think through how the teacher might react and what your response will be.

- Review the goals of the observation. Review with the teacher the focus you both agreed on and how you structured your observation. Keep the conversation focused throughout the conference. It will be easy to slip into a conversation about a sick child or the teacher's stressful life, but these topics will only divert attention from the teacher's development as a science teacher. You will have to be the judge when circumstances are important enough to modify the agenda.

- Open with an opportunity for the teacher to comment. Establish the value you place on the teacher's thinking by asking the following questions: "What did you think about the activities I observed?" "Were you pleased with how things went?" "Did you think your goals for the children's engagement and science learning were achieved?" Listen carefully to the responses. The teacher's perspective will give important clues as to how you proceed.

- Share your observations. Start by acknowledging places where you agree with the teacher, making specific connections between the teaching you observed and children's responses. Note the places where your perceptions might differ.

- Use available documentation to describe and analyze the events observed. Any documentation you have is data that can be analyzed. Use these documents to illustrate the descriptive points you and the teacher are making. Note the discrepancies in your perceptions and the teacher's, and what stands out in the data. As you begin to analyze the observed events, consider any discrepancies, the teacher's goals for the children, and the focus of her work with you. You want the teacher to do most of the talking, synthesizing her own impressions and your observations in order to assess her growth and needs. Use statements and questions to guide her reflection. Consider pursuing the following:

  - What the data says about the focus of her work with you—"You are working on strategies for facilitating science talks. What strategies did you effectively use in this activity?" "Let's look at the data and see what the children's responses were." Proceed to analyze the teacher's strategies in relation to the children's responses.

  - What the data says about student engagement and learning—"Let's look at this information and think about the science concepts being explored." Once identified, ask about evidence of the children's interests, questions, and understandings in relation to those particular concepts. Create a picture of the children's current understandings, their questions, and particular interests.

  - What the data highlights or the discrepancies in your perceptions—"I was amazed to see how much more Margarita is talking. What do you think has contributed to her new ability to participate in science talks and to the vocabulary she is using?" "We seem to have different ideas about how the children can control flowing water and why. You are seeing some behaviors intended to speed up and slow down the flow that I didn't notice. I would like to better understand your thinking. Can you be more specific about what you have seen?"

- Help the teacher plan next steps for her teaching and the children's learning. Once you have analyzed the observation, it is time to think about the implications for her teaching. You will want her to determine her next steps with the children and what she will do next in relation to the objectives she is working on.

  Start with the following questions: "What do you think your next steps should be with these children? How can you extend this experience and build their science understanding? What would you want to accomplish with these strategies? Why do you think these are the right next steps? How will they elevate the science and promote inquiry?"

- Close with goal setting and planning. It is now time to plan the teacher's next professional development steps. Should she continue to work on this goal? It is best to stay with one focus for a while, allowing the teacher to fully integrate new strategies and experience their effect. When it is time to move on to a new goal, select appropriate objectives. Finally, plan a few activities that will help her move forward. You might give her an article to read or suggest a classroom for her to observe. Her plans might simply be trying out things in her classroom. Once plans are made, record them on a teacher development plan (p. 211 in "Resources"), synthesize the major points of the conversation, and schedule your follow-up.

resources

Key Instructional Strategies

As you conduct the basic and advanced workshops, you will use four key instructional strategies:

- Encourage exploration of water

- Facilitate reflection on the science in teachers' explorations

- Present content about science and science teaching

- Guide analysis of classroom documentation to create a bridge between theory and practice

When these strategies are interwoven throughout your training program, you will help teachers integrate the *Exploring Water with Young Children* approach into their teaching practice. In these workshops exploration precedes the presentation of content so that teachers can connect the content to these recent experiences with water and inquiry. When the analysis follows the science and science teaching content, it provides oppor-

tunities to make the content presented practical. Below we describe each strategy, providing a purpose for its use and guidelines to follow as you use them in your training program. In addition, you will find strategies for effectively using the video vignettes.

ENCOURAGE EXPLORATION

These hands-on experiences provide adults with the opportunity to engage in inquiry and model, at an adult level, the children's investigations and experiences with water. They provide direct experiences with inquiry-based teaching through an open exploration of water, focused investigations of flow, drops, sinking and floating, representation, and data collection and analysis.

PURPOSE

- Review past experiences with water and draw connections to new understandings

- Experience the use of inquiry skills and science exploration in the same way the children will

- Begin to build understanding of the science concepts, the nature of inquiry, and the approach to teaching

GUIDANCE

- Your preparation is key to effective training. You will want to read the advance preparation instructions at the beginning of each workshop. The preparation will involve exploring water and collecting the materials for the exploration. Read "Step 1: Preparing Yourself—Science" in the teacher's guide (p. 13) to help you understand the concepts that are the focus of these water explorations.

- As you lead teacher-explorers, you will be modeling the approach to teaching described in the teacher's guide, although you will discuss the science at an adult level as described in the trainer's guide. Use the teacher's guide as a resource as you prepare and reflect on your teaching. In the instructions for the workshops you will find discussion questions and purpose statements that will help you maintain your teachers' focus.

- The time frame we have created is our best estimate of how much time you will need. Feel free to adjust it, based on your style and the needs and interests of your participants. However, it is important not to skip any of the activities, as the exploration will have little meaning without the reflection, content, and analysis pieces or vice versa.

- Support everyone's engagement. As you observe what is happening during the hands-on explorations, be sure that everyone is engaged. Look for the participants who are hanging back or being dominated by another group member. Engage them by asking them what they have noticed or suggest a job they could perform for the group.

FACILITATE REFLECTION

These large group conversations involve discussion of and reflection on the group's experiences during their explorations—group experiences provide the opportunity to learn from one another and draw conclusions from a much larger body of evidence. Teachers will have time to process their experiences in the same way they will do it with children, draw conclusions from the work of the whole group, and build an understanding of the power of reflection and collaborative thinking.

PURPOSE

- Connect the explorations to the underlying science concepts and inquiry skills

- Connect the explorations to the teachers' own teaching and their children's learning

- Articulate the teachers' current understandings

GUIDANCE

- Listen carefully. You will be learning a lot about teachers' current understandings of the science content and their teaching of science. Note confusions that you will need to address now or follow up on later. Modify your future interactions to respond to teachers' needs and interests, just as you would with children.

- Prompt teachers for fuller descriptions and explanations. You will help them expand their understanding as well as learn more about their thinking if you pursue a comment or question before moving on to the next one. Ask, "What happened? Where did the water go? How would you describe its flow?"

- Maintain the focus. Keep your ultimate goal in mind—to prepare teachers to use *Exploring Water with Young Children* successfully in their classrooms. Each reflective conversation has an instructional purpose and a limited amount of time. Try to manage the time so teachers have an opportunity to discuss all of the important reflection questions.

PRESENT CONTENT

This strategy is your opportunity to formally share content. The content will be about science concepts and inquiry skills, specifics about *Exploring Water with Young Children* and its approach, or descriptions of the teachers' roles. Presentations are supported by overheads and references to sections of the teacher's guide.

PURPOSE

- Begin to understand the *Exploring Water with Young Children* approach to science teaching and learning

- Become familiar with the teacher's guide and the many resources it contains

GUIDANCE

- Use the visual and print material that support these presentations. The references to the teacher's guide are important resources for teachers. By referring to them in your presentations, you help teachers learn when and how to use them. The overheads will also help your visual learners stay engaged throughout the presentations.

- Make connections between the content of the presentations and the teachers' past experiences with water or the classroom water table (for example, when you are talking about observing children's explorations, ask teachers which strategies they have successfully used in the past to document observations). When these connections are explicit it will be easier for teachers to absorb the content.

GUIDE ANALYSIS

While the explorations and presentations are important, they will only have an impact on practice when teachers can make connections between what they are learning and their work as teachers. To help them make these connections, engage them in analyzing classroom documentation (such as the video vignettes, children's work samples, teachers' journal entries, and photographs).

PURPOSE

- Connect science content and science teaching to daily work with young children
- Build skill as reflective, analytical thinkers
- Learn to see the science ideas and inquiry skills in the many forms of children's communication
- Build the ability to use documentation when assessing their own science teaching as well as the children's science learning

GUIDANCE

- Familiarize yourself with the criteria in this guide that are being used to analyze each document or vignette. For example, you will want to review the content that is important for the analysis of each video vignette before looking at the tape. If you are going to be looking at children's inquiry, review the inquiry diagram and inquiry skills outcomes.
- Begin with description and move to analysis. Good analysis is built on clear ideas about what is being analyzed. Begin these conversations with a description of the documentation—observations of the behaviors and interactions on a video vignette or descriptions of the elements of a child's work sample. Ask guiding questions to help par-

ticipants describe their observations, and then help them make connections to the criteria being used for analysis. For example, describing the characteristics of the drops represented in a drawing helps teachers to think about what the child has and hasn't noticed. Then, the teacher can think about what this means. Specifically, they can ask themselves, "Now that I have a better understanding of what this child knows, what does that mean for my next steps as a teacher?"

- Monitor small group conversations. When teachers are working in small groups, listen to the conversations around the room. You will gain insight into groups' thinking and can troubleshoot with those groups that get off track. Interject a comment or a question to move a group forward or sit down and facilitate their conversation for a while.
- Remember the science content and inquiry skills. Each classroom artifact or video vignette provides another opportunity for insight into the science content. As teachers see the science concepts reflected in various ways on video or in children's work samples, they will deepen their understanding of these science concepts and the inquiry process.

USING THE VIDEO VIGNETTES

Video vignettes have a special role in *Exploring Water with Young Children* training. They provide a unique opportunity for teachers to see the science teaching and learning of other early childhood classrooms. While doing this, teachers begin to think analytically, connecting what they have learned about the *Exploring Water with Young Children* approach to actual classroom work.

The teachers shown in these vignettes are at different stages of development as science teachers and vary in their teaching style. They all use important strategies and engage their children in an exploration of water, but they all miss opportunities as well. Use these vignettes to draw out important aspects of science teaching and learning, and to identify other approaches that would also be effective. The point is not to criticize or defend the teachers, but to use their work as a stimulus for talking about science teaching and learning.

Each vignette has been selected for a particular purpose, but they also present an opportunity to think about the science concepts in a classroom setting. Use questions that draw out the science present in the video in addition to the other things you want your participants to see—"What science was being explored here?" Reinforce the link between the teaching and the learning—"Why do you think the teacher did that? What did the children gain? How did it focus children's thinking on a science idea? How did it promote inquiry?" Also ask for specifics. Return to the video to show segments again to be sure everyone agrees—"Where did you see evidence of that? What was the child doing? What was the teacher doing?"

Use the vignettes more than once. There is a lot to see and think about and teachers will benefit from multiple viewings. Use them in guided discussions, or allow teachers to take them home or look at them with their colleagues. Provide guiding questions that give focus to the viewing. Use the vignette log that follows to plan ways of using each vignette so that it meets teachers' needs.

Video Vignette Log

> The workshop instructions provide additional information about each of these vignettes, including the following: key science concepts being explored, inquiry skills being used, and teacher strategies. The workshops also provide guidance for discussing the vignettes. If you are using a vignette with individual teachers or as part of a guided discussion, be sure to review relevant sections about the vignettes in the workshops and sessions in which they are used.

1. INTRODUCTION (7 minutes 21 seconds)

This montage presents a view of the culture of inquiry in classrooms where the children are engaged in exploring water. They are using varied materials to examine how water appears in containers and flows from one to another. They are pursuing questions about how to adjust the flow of water and how drops will appear on different surfaces. They are carefully observing the impact of their actions and discussing what their experiences tell them about the properties of water. These teachers are observing children, identifying their questions, and facilitating their inquiry.

Such snapshots illustrate what children's in-depth, inquiry-based exploration of water looks like and the teacher's role as a guide. This montage, which serves as an excellent introduction to *Exploring Water with Young Children*, is used in the first workshop, and the first advanced workshop, "Creating a Culture of Inquiry about Exploring Water." It might also be used for introducing families and community groups to *Exploring Water with Young Children*.

2. FOCUSED EXPLORATION OF WATER FLOW (4 minutes 1 second)

This vignette, filmed at a Boston class for four- and five-year-olds, shows three children at the water table. One girl is exploring the flow of water through a tube set in a water wall and the two boys are working with basters, learning how to get the water in and out again.

This vignette is used in workshop 2: "Getting Ready" and workshop 5: "Overview of Focused Exploration." It might also be used to:

- Practice observing children's engagement and analyzing their understandings

- Have a more in-depth discussion of the teacher's role in promoting children's science inquiry, by considering the next steps she might take

3. OPEN EXPLORATION OF WATER (3 minutes 45 seconds)

This vignette, filmed in a Boston Head Start classroom, shows a group of four preschool children at the water table. The teacher joins them and encourages them to notice what the water is doing.

This vignette is used in workshop 3: "Overview of Open Exploration." It might also be used to:

- Engage in a deeper analysis of the teacher's role, asking, "How might this teacher bring the science forward? What would next steps be for these children's inquiry?"

4. EXPLORING SINKING AND FLOATING
(7 minutes 7 seconds)

This vignette, filmed in a Connecticut early childhood program, shows a teacher and a small group of children engaged in a focused exploration of sinking and floating. The vignette shows the teacher introducing the activity, the children's exploration, documentation of their findings, and a discussion of what they learned.

This vignette is used in basic workshop 7: "Focused Exploration of Sinking and Floating" and workshop 14: "Facilitating Science Talks." It might also be used to:

- Practice observation of children with varying abilities and understandings

- Have a more in-depth discussion of the teacher's role in promoting children's science inquiry and how it reflects strategies discussed in "The Teacher's Role," which appears in the teacher's guide

- Consider next steps the teacher might take and how their investigation of enclosures might proceed

5. MAKING BUBBLES (4 minutes 30 seconds)

In this vignette, filmed at a Boston class of four- and five-year-olds, four children are discovering ways they can produce bubbles in water. The teacher helps them articulate their observations and the process they are engaged in. She shows a value for listening to others and sharing discoveries.

This vignette is used in workshop 9: "Deepening Children's Science Understandings" and workshop 11: "Assessing Children's Science Learning." It might also be used to:

- Consider how the vignette exemplifies focused exploration and/or strategies suggested in "The Teacher's Role."

- Consider next steps the teacher might take, including other ways to explore bubbles and discuss their observations and what they have learned from them, leading toward some generalizations about air in water.

6. FOCUSED EXPLORATION OF DROPS
(7 minutes 7 seconds)

In this vignette, four children are engaged in a focused exploration of drops. The teacher introduces the activity, and then the children make predictions and try out drops on different surfaces, and represent and discuss what they have learned.

This vignette is used in workshop 12: "Encouraging Representation" and workshop 13: "Using Children's Representations as Teaching Tools." It might also be used to:

- Practice observation of children with varying abilities and understandings

- Discuss ways a teacher can build connections from one activity to another—connecting previous exploration to today's exploration and today's exploration to representation and discussion.

7. TALKING ABOUT MOVING WATER
(4 minutes 1 second)

This vignette was filmed at a Boston class of four- and five-year-olds, the same classroom as "Making Bubbles." Two children are sharing their approach to moving water through a tube with the whole class. The teacher uses props, the children's representations, and strategic questions to help facilitate the sharing.

This vignette is used in workshop 15: "Facilitating Science Talks." The vignette might also be used to:

- Discuss using children's representations as teaching tools

- Discuss children's science understandings and how they are reflected in their language and representational work

- Think about what the next steps might be for these children

GUIDED DISCUSSION PLANS: SAMPLE 1

This beginning-level discussion, which focuses on understanding the *Exploring Water with Young Children* teacher's guide, might be used with teachers who have only participated in the basic workshops. Others like it might follow and focus on other aspects of the teacher's guide.

OBJECTIVES

To better understand the open exploration section of the teacher's guide.
- What is the purpose of open exploration and what does the children's activity look like?
- What does the teacher do during open exploration?

CONTENT

Ask teachers to read the open exploration section of the guide. Begin the meeting by listing key points about open exploration with the teachers.

DOCUMENT MATERIALS

Video cued to vignette 3 or a video created in one of your classrooms.

SAMPLE DISCUSSION QUESTIONS

Describe: What did you see in this video? How would you describe the children's engagement? What about the teacher's actions?

Analyze: Why do you think the teacher called the children's attention to the speed of the water? How does it exemplify open exploration? What other connections can you see between the video and our list?

Prompt: Can you explain what you mean? How does that connect to the science concepts? How does it encourage inquiry? Or, what is the connection there?

Conclude: What does this mean for your teaching? What do you think you will do differently next week? Why? What do you want to accomplish with your students? How will you do that? How will you know when you have accomplished that? What evidence will you look for?

GUIDED DISCUSSION PLANS: SAMPLE 2

A discussion, like this one, that highlights a particular aspect of children's learning, can happen at any time. It builds on a teacher's understanding after the basic or advanced workshops, providing new insight through analysis of a new stimulus or by reviewing a stimulus they are familiar with from a new perspective.

OBJECTIVES

To better understand inquiry and what it looks like when children are exploring the properties of water.

- What is inquiry?
- What aspects of inquiry are three-, four-, or five-year-olds capable of engaging in?
- How does a teacher help children engage in inquiry?

CONTENT

Use the inquiry diagram and description from the teacher's guide. Review key points, writing them on a chart at the beginning of the meeting.

DOCUMENT MATERIALS

Excerpts from a teacher's journal (pp. 10–12 in the teacher's guide), video cued to vignettes 5 or 6, or a video vignette or series of photographs from one of your classrooms.

SAMPLE DISCUSSION QUESTIONS

Describe: What exactly did you see the children doing in this video vignette?

Prompt: Help them focus on a particular child by asking questions like, "And what was Linda doing?" Be sure they stick to describing the behavior, not analyzing the inquiry.

Analyze: Which inquiry skills were being used? Which science ideas were being explored?

Prompt: Can you explain why you think so? What did the teacher do to extend this experience with bubbles? Why do you think she did that? How do you think that influenced the children's thinking? What evidence was there of that? What understandings about science were evident? Where?

Conclude: What does this mean for your teaching? What do you think you will do differently next week? Why? What do you want to accomplish with your children? How will you do that? How will you know that you have succeeded?

GUIDED DISCUSSION PLANS: SAMPLE 3

This discussion, which could span several meetings, helps teachers connect their teaching to children's learning. It should come after the teachers are well grounded in the *Exploring Water with Young Children* approach and are refining their science teaching.

OBJECTIVES

To better understand how children use representation to reflect their science ideas.

- Recognize children's science ideas in representations where they have used various media.
- Select appropriate media, considering topic and children's diverse capacities.
- Use assessment of children's work to plan next steps.

CONTENT

Important ideas, video vignettes, and work samples from the two workshops on representation (advanced workshops 12 and 13).

DOCUMENT MATERIALS

Selected samples of children's work using different media from your classrooms or from workshops.

SAMPLE DISCUSSION QUESTIONS

Describe: Talk about samples one at a time. What do you see in this drawing? What characteristics of the drops has Megan focused on with the clay?

Prompt: How has she used shape to represent drops? How has she used size? Repeat for several samples, varying child ability or media.

Analyze children's work: How do these samples differ?

Prompt: What is the evidence for how they differ?

Analyze teaching: What have these representation experiences contributed to the children's inquiry? Do these media help children think about the science and communicate their ideas? What other media might be used with these children? How might you use this document in the classroom?

Prompt: Have you tried that media? Why do you think it will work here? What specifically would you do? What response would you hope for?

Conclude: What does this mean for your teaching? What do you think you will do differently next week? Why? What do you want to accomplish with your children? How will you do that?

GUIDED DISCUSSION PLANNING FORM

Name: _____

Date: _____

Goal: _____

Objective(s): _____

Pre-reading: _____

Content Focus: _____

Stimulus: _____

Questions that encourage description:

Questions that stimulate analysis:

Concluding questions:

Your reflection on the discussion:

1. Describe the engagement of the teachers in this discussion. What insights did they share as they analyzed the stimulus material? What do they understand? What are their questions?

2. How would you evaluate the effectiveness of the discussion? Consider the appropriateness of the goal, objective(s), materials, and questions. What worked? What would you do differently next time?

3. What are appropriate next steps for these teachers? Do they need more time on this topic or are they ready for a new one? If you are moving to a new one, what will it be? Have the teachers given input into this decision? How might you involve them? Is there potential leadership emerging? How will you nurture it?

Assessing Teacher Growth

Taking time periodically to assess teachers' growth will help you respond to their professional development interests and needs. Assessment will be especially helpful when you are moving from the basic to advanced workshops and when you are planning mentoring or guided discussions. Use the following two tools:

- Science Teacher Development Stages—Describes knowledge and skills at three stages of development as inquiry-based science teachers. Professional development goals are suggested for each stage. Refer to these stages when you have assessment data and want to plan appropriate next steps.

- Evaluating Science Teaching—A tool for recording your observations of teacher practice. Use it to gather evidence on which to base decisions about next steps in professional development. Planning advanced workshops, guided discussions, and mentoring are all times when this information will be helpful. You might also want to use it to chart teachers' progress, adding evidence as teachers develop new skills. You will find some additional guidance on using this form at the end of the section on science teacher development stages.

SCIENCE TEACHER DEVELOPMENT STAGES

Your teachers will go through a developmental process as they learn to use *Exploring Water with Young Children*. This process can be defined in three stages: beginning, developing, and refining. Most teachers will likely start as beginners because they have very little experience facilitating an in-depth study of science with young children. Both the content and process of this type of science teaching will be new to them. While the approach to teaching science is new, it is assumed that they have a base in child development and developmentally appropriate practices that will inform their work as science teachers.

Understanding your teachers' current knowledge and skills will help you plan appropriate professional development and set realistic goals with individual teachers, as they will progress through these stages at different rates.

THE TEACHER BEGINNING TO USE *EXPLORING WATER WITH YOUNG CHILDREN*

- Current Knowledge and Skills—The beginning teacher is unfamiliar with many of the approaches used in *Exploring Water with Young Children*. If she has experience in teaching science at all it may be setting up a science table, conducting isolated activities, or implementing themes that are rotated on a weekly or biweekly basis.

- Appropriate Goals for Teachers Beginning to Use *Exploring Water with Young Children*—Teachers beginning to use *Exploring Water with Young Children* will focus on following the step-by-step instructions in the curriculum guides. Possible goals include the following:

  - Beginning to understand the purpose, flow, and activities in the teacher's guide

  - Gaining a basic understanding of the science concepts being explored and the role of inquiry in science teaching and learning

  - Creating the environment as described in the teacher's guide, including materials, sufficient time, and space

  - Engaging children in the exploration and supporting their inquiry

  - Beginning to document children's science experiences

THE TEACHER DEVELOPING HER SCIENCE PRACTICE

- Current Knowledge and Skills—The developing teacher may still struggle with some of the same things the beginning teacher is experiencing, for example, how to get all of the children engaged. But she understands the goals, values the approach, and has some ability to engage children in inquiry-based science. Science engagement will be evident in the environment and interactions in this classroom. The children's interactions and the classroom displays will reveal a focus on water exploration. The developing teacher acknowledges children's science explorations and creates opportunities for children to reflect on experiences and ideas through discussion and representation.

- Appropriate Goals—The developing teacher is beginning to focus on improving her science teaching and promoting children's science learning. Possible goals include the following:

    - Continuing to build understanding of the purpose, flow, and activities in the teacher's guide

    - Building a deeper understanding of the science concepts and how young children build their theories and ideas

    - Creating a more "science rich" environment, including displays and accessible books that inform and stimulate investigation

    - Developing the ability to facilitate children's inquiry, balancing exploration with conversation and representation

    - Learning to use teacher's and children's documentation to stimulate inquiry and to connect children's day-to-day science activities

    - Learning to observe, document, and assess children's science engagement and learning

THE TEACHER REFINING HER SCIENCE PRACTICE

- Current Knowledge and Skills—The refining teacher continues to develop her skills and abilities in all of the areas of the developing teacher and may still struggle with some of the same issues. For example, facilitating science talks that are focused on science experiences and ideas or understanding the science more deeply might continue to be challenging. But this teacher is comfortable with her use of the curriculum, the science concepts, and many of the teaching strategies. She uses documentation and reflection to guide her own development. She adapts her teaching, which is based on her understandings of the responses and needs of individual children as well as the whole group. Evidence of water exploration permeates the classroom. The environment has many examples of children's work, water centers with various investigations going on, and opportunities for small and large group science talks.

- Appropriate Goals—This teacher is focused on building the link between her teaching and the

children's science learning. Possible goals include the following:

- Using all parts of the teacher's guide to develop a system for observation, documentation, assessment, and planning

- Building a deeper understanding of the science concepts being explored and how children's understanding is expressed in their behaviors and comments

- Creating an environment that reflects children's current investigations

- Developing the ability to deepen science thinking through interactions with children

- Using documents more effectively to encourage children's reflection and further investigations

- Integrating *Exploring Water with Young Children* with math, language, literacy, and social goals

- Describing children's science engagement and learning to families and others

- Extending the exploration beyond the teacher's guide or developing explorations of new topics

EVALUATING SCIENCE TEACHING

On p. 206 you will find a tool to guide your evaluation of teachers. Use it when conducting observations of each teacher to determine appropriate professional development and set goals for individual work. You might also want to use it to chart teachers' progress, adding evidence as teachers develop new skills. An observation is unlikely to provide all of the information you need to complete the evaluation. Arrange for a conference with the teacher and discuss what you have observed and some of the things you have not seen, for example, her observational notes or her work with her assistant or volunteers.

Different sections of the form are relevant for evaluating teachers at each stage of development. As teachers become more skilled, you will want to expand the aspects of their practice that you are focusing on. Use the following guidance when planning your observations:

- When evaluating beginning teachers, focus on sections I A, B, and C; II A 1 and 2; II B 1.

- When evaluating developing teachers, continue to focus on the sections that you used for the beginning teacher and add sections: I D and the rest of II.

- When evaluating refining teachers, use the whole form.

EVALUATING SCIENCE TEACHING

Teacher(s): _____

Date: _____

Observer: _____

Teacher

Behaviors	Evidence
A. Teacher uses *Exploring Water* teacher's guide to structure and sequence meaningful science explorations	
1. Follows steps in teacher's guide, using the teaching cycle of engage, explore, and reflect.	
B. Teacher uses environment to stimulate science exploration	
1. Provides materials and tools for explorations as described in *Exploring Water* teacher's guide.	
2. Provides variety of two- and three-dimensional representational materials.	
3. Displays materials and books for easy access by children.	
4. Arranges furniture so children have enough room to work around the water table and at other water centers in groups of three to five.	
5. Creates displays at children's eye level that provide valuable information, relate to current science interests, and show children's own work.	
6. Provides choice times (thirty to forty-five minutes) with opportunities for children to engage with the science materials.	

Evaluating Science Teaching (cont'd)

Behaviors	Evidence
C. Teacher gives attention and positive encouragement to help children focus on science explorations	
1. Uses comments and questions to acknowledge activity and elicit ideas. Listens with genuine interest.	
2. Engages with children, modeling curiosity, play behavior, and use of tools. Invites reluctant explorers to play and helps them manage frustration by engaging them in problem solving.	
D. Teacher uses strategies that deepen children's science understanding and engage them in inquiry	
1. Encourages children's inquiry—observation, questioning, data collection, recording, and analysis. Offers new challenges as children are ready.	
2. Provides materials in varied media for children to represent an aspect of their experience or a developing theory and encourages the children to represent.	
3. Finds ways to focus children on science in their play.	
4. Facilitates science talks in which children share their experiences, ideas, theories, and conclusions.	
E. Teacher systematically observes and documents for assessment and teaching purposes	
1. Documents observations and interactions using various media, such as observation records, photos, audiotape and videotape, and collected work samples.	
2. Uses documents as teaching tools to connect day-to-day activities, stimulate and bring thinking forward, and launch new challenges.	

Children

Behaviors	Evidence
A. Children are engaged	
1. Use varied materials to explore water, gaining a basic understanding of its properties.	
2. Talk to each other and the adults about their science explorations.	
3. Engage in inquiry: observing, questioning, collecting data, recording, reflecting, and constructing explanations.	
4. Represent a part of their explorations—drawing, using collage materials or clay, or using their bodies to represent their work and scientific knowledge.	
5. Use resources (peers, books, Web sites, and so on) to extend their explorations and gain new information.	
B. Children are motivated and persistent	
1. Are eager to use the areas of the classroom that are designed for science explorations.	
2. Bring in items or tell stories from home that relate to their explorations.	
3. Show enthusiasm and interest extending to lunch table conversation, request reading from books and for dramatic play, and so on.	

Going Deeper

Behaviors	Evidence

A. Teacher helps other adults learn how to support children's science explorations

1. Supports assistant(s) in developing their ability to encourage children's science explorations.

2. Finds specific roles for classroom volunteers that support children's science explorations.

3. When opportunities arise, serves as a mentor to beginning science teachers.

B. Teacher extends own understanding of science and expands classroom applications

1. Extends this exploration beyond the steps in the teacher's guide.

2. Develops explorations of new topics.

3. Teacher seeks out deeper understanding of science content.

SCIENCE TEACHER OBSERVATION SYNTHESIS

Teacher: _____

Date: _____

Current goal/objective of teacher: _____

Teacher's goals for science and inquiry in observed activity

Children's Behavior/Comments	Teacher's Response

Questions or points to consider with teacher

SCIENCE TEACHER DEVELOPMENT PLAN

Teacher: _____

Date: _____

Strengths as a science teacher:

One goal for growth as a science teacher:

Objectives:

Activity	Time Frame	Resources Needed

Follow-up: (what and when)

References

Science and Teaching Resources for Instructors

See resource list for teachers below for additional titles. Note that the teacher resources are also valuable for instructors, and instructors should read all readings before giving them to teachers. You might also want to share some of these instructor resources with your teachers.

Bowman, Barbara, ed. 2000. *Eager to learn: Educating our preschoolers*. Washington, D.C.: National Academy Press.

DeVries, R., et al. 2002. *Developing constructivist early childhood curriculum*. New York: Teachers College Press.

Gallas, Karen. 1995. *Talking their way into science*. New York: Teachers College Press.

Goldhaber, Jeanne, and Dee Smith. 1997. You look at things differently: The role of documentation in the professional development of a campus child care center staff. *Early Childhood Education Journal* 25 (1): 3–10.

Harlen, W. 2001. *Primary science: Taking the plunge*. Portsmouth, N.H.: Heinemann.

Landry, Christopher E., and George E. Forman. 1999. Research on early science education. In *The early childhood curriculum: Current findings in theory and practice*. New York: Teachers College Press.

Lind, Karen. 1996. *Exploring science in early childhood: A developmental approach*. 2d ed. Albany, N.Y.: Delmar Publishers.

Lindfors, Judith W. 1999. *Children's inquiry: Using language to make sense of the world*. New York: Teachers College Press.

Moriarty, Robin F. 2002. Helping teachers develop as facilitators of three- to five-year-olds' science inquiry. Entries from a staff developer's journal. *Young Children* 57 (5): 20–24.

Osborne, Roger, and Peter Freyberg. 1985. *Learning in science: The implications of children's science*. Portsmouth, N.H.: Heinemann.

Perry, Gail, and Mary Rivkin. 1992. Teachers and science. *Young Children* 47 (4): 9–16.

Project 2061—Science for All Americans. 1999. *Dialogue on early childhood science, mathematics and technology education*. Washington, D.C.: American Association for the Advancement of Science.

Schweinhart, Larry J., and David P. Weikart. 1998. Why curriculum matters in early childhood education. *Educational Leadership* 55 (6): 57–60.

Wasserman, Selma, and J. W. George Ivany. 1996. *Who's afraid of spiders? The new teaching elementary science*. 2d ed. New York: Teachers College Press.

Science and Teaching Resources for Teachers

Cadwell, Louise B., and Brenda V. Fyfe. 1997. Conversations with children. In *First steps toward teaching the Reggio way*, edited by J. Hendrick. Upper Saddle River, N.J.: Merrill/Prentice Hall.

Chaille, Christine, and Lory Britain. 2003. *The young child as scientist: A constructivist approach to early childhood science education*. New York: Allyn & Bacon.

Copley, Juanita V. 2000. *The young child and mathematics*. Washington, D.C.: National Association for the Education of Young Children (NAEYC).

Doris, Ellen. 1991. *Doing what scientists do: Children learn to investigate their world*. Portsmouth, N.H.: Heinemann.

Feynman, Richard P. 1988. The making of a scientist. In *What do you care what other people think?* New York: W.W. Norton.

Forman, George. 1996. A child constructs an understanding of a water wheel in five media. *Childhood Education* 72 (5): 269–273.

———. 1996. Helping children ask good questions. In *The Wonder of It*, edited by B. Neugebauer. Redmond, Wash.: Exchange Press.

———. 1996. Negotiating with art media to deepen learning. *Child Care Information Exchange* 108: 56–58.

Harlan, Jean. 1992. *Science experiences for the early childhood years*. 5th ed. New York: Macmillan Publishing Company.

Hirsch, Elisabeth S., ed. 1996. *The block book*. Washington, D.C.: NAEYC.

Hoisington, Cynthia. 2002. Using photographs to support children's science inquiry. *Young Children* 57 (5): 26–30.

Kostelnik, Marjorie. 1992. Myths associated with developmentally appropriate programs. *Young Children* 47 (4): 17–23.

McIntyre, Margaret. 1984. *Early childhood and science*. Washington, D.C.: National Science Teachers Association.

NAEYC. 1998. Learning to read and write: Developmentally appropriate practices for young children. *Young Children* 53 (4): 30–46.

Osborne, Roger, and Peter Freyberg. 1985. *Learning in science: The implications of children's science.* Portsmouth, N.H.: Heinemann.

Owens, Caroline. 1999. Conversational science 101A: Talking it up! *Young Children* 54 (5): 4–9.

Shepardson, D. P., and S. J. Britsch. 2000. Analyzing children's science journals. *Science and Children* 38 (3): 29–33.

Smith, N. R. 1998. *Observation drawing with children: A framework for teachers.* New York: Teachers College Press.

Sprung, Barbara. 1996. Physics is fun, physics is important, and physics belongs in the early childhood classroom. *Young Children* 51 (5): 29–33.

Tudge, Jonathan, and David Caruso. 1988. Cooperative problem-solving in the classroom: Enhancing young children's cognitive development. *Young Children* 44 (1): 46–52.

Worth, K., and S. Grollmar. 2003. *Worms, shadows, and whirlpools: Science in early childhood classrooms.* Portsmouth, N.H.: Heinemann, and Washington, D.C.: NAEYC.

Yinger, J., and S. Blaszka. 1995. A year of journaling— A year of building with young children. *Young Children.* 51 (1): 15–20.

index